I0214694

# The Christ of the Gospels

by

Henry Clay Morrison

*First Fruits Press*
*Wilmore, Kentucky*
*c2015*

*The Christ of the Gospels*, by Henry Clay Morrison

First Fruits Press, ©2015

Previously published by the Pentecostal Publishing Company, ©1926

ISBN: 9781621712237 (print), 9781621712244 (digital), 9781621712251(kindle)

http://place.asburyseminary.edu/firstfruitsheritagematerial/112/

First Fruits Press is a digital imprint of the Asbury Theological Seminary, B.L. Fisher Library. Asbury Theological Seminary is the legal owner of the material previously published by the Pentecostal Publishing Co. and reserves the right to release new editions of this material as well as new material produced by Asbury Theological Seminary. Its publications are available for noncommercial and educational uses, such as research, teaching and private study. First Fruits Press has licensed the digital version of this work under the Creative Commons Attribution Noncommercial 3.0 United States License. To view a copy of this license, visit http://creativecommons.org/licenses/by-nc/3.0/us/.

For all other uses, contact:

First Fruits Press
B.L. Fisher Library
Asbury Theological Seminary
204 N. Lexington Ave.
Wilmore, KY 40390
http://place.asburyseminary.edu/firstfruits

Morrison, Henry Clay 1857-1942.
   Christ of the Gospels / by Henry Clay Morrison.
   103 pages ; 21 cm.
   Wilmore, Ky. : First Fruits Press, ©2015.
   Reprint. Previously published: Louisville, KY : Pentecostal Publishing
   Company ©1926.
   ISBN:9781621712237 (pbk.)
   1. Jesus Christ -- Sermons. 2. Sermons, American. I. Title.
BX8333.M6 C5 2015                                                                      252

Cover design by John Ramsey

asburyseminary.edu
800.2ASBURY
204 North Lexington Avenue
Wilmore, Kentucky 40390

*First Fruits*
THE ACADEMIC OPEN PRESS OF ASBURY SEMINARY

First Fruits Press
*The Academic Open Press of Asbury Theological Seminary*
204 N. Lexington Ave., Wilmore, KY 40390
859-858-2236
first.fruits@asburyseminary.edu
asbury.to/firstfruits

# THE CHRIST
# OF THE GOSPELS

HENRY CLAY MORRISON

# The Christ of the Gospels

By

## HENRY CLAY MORRISON

*Author of "Sermons for the Times," "The
Second Coming of Christ," etc.*

PENTECOSTAL PUBLISHING COMPANY
Incorporated
LOUISVILLE, KY.

Copyright, MCMXXVI, by
FLEMING H. REVELL COMPANY

*To the Children of God who believe His Word, and trust in His Son, Jesus Christ, for Redemption, and look to the Holy Spirit for guidance and keeping power.*

# PREFACE

MOST of the sermons in this book have been preached in revival meetings, and at the great camp-meetings throughout the nation, and have been blessed of God in helping to lead many souls to salvation through faith in Christ.

A large number of my friends in many parts of the country have insisted that I have them published in book form.

I am having them published, and am sending them forth with the prayer and hope that they may prove helpful to all those who may read them. I am growing old, and have a desire that this book may carry a message of salvation to hungry human hearts long after I have ceased to speak.

I want the contents of this book to bear witness through the years to my undying faith in the Lord Jesus Christ as my personal and all-sufficient Saviour.

There sermons are but a poor expression of some of the great truths of that Gospel which is the power of God unto salvation. May the Holy Spirit illuminate the minds of those who may read the contents of this book, to discover in our blessed Lord Jesus one able to save to the uttermost all who come to Him.

H. C. M.

*Louisville, Ky.*

# CONTENTS

# I

# THE CHRIST OF THE GOSPELS

*" Without controversy great is the mystery of godliness: God was manifest in the flesh, justified in the Spirit, seen of angels, preached unto the Gentiles, believed on in the world, received up into glory."*—1 TIMOTHY 3: 16.

THE inspired writers nowhere undertake to explain the mysteries which abound in the revelations God has made to men. It must be understood that the revelation of the divine Being —the incarnation of Jesus Christ—and the new and holy life of peace and joy which comes to those who trust in Him cannot be figured out and explained by mathematical processes or in terms of human philosophy. We would call attention to the fact that it is not necessary to enter the realm of divine revelation and our Christian religion in order to find mysteries; we are surrounded with mysteries. There are many things with which we come in constant contact which we cannot understand. Who can explain to us electricity? We know it exists; it is about us everywhere; it illuminates our pathway with its light; its penetrating rays may destroy germs and heal us of disease. We may cook our food with its heat. It leaps across the ocean carrying our message with the speed of lightning, but Edison himself cannot tell us what electricity is.

Professor Huxley once wrote: " The mysteries of the Church are child's play compared with the mysteries of nature. The doctrine of the trinity is no more puzzling than the necessary antinomies of physical speculation; virgin procreation and resuscitation from apparent death are ordinary phenomenon for the naturalist." If men propose to reject what they cannot understand, they will have to reject not only the mysteries of the spiritual world, but the mysteries of the natural world as well, for all nature about us is full of problems that have not been solved.

"Great is the mystery of godliness." Angels at the present time are doubtless far more intelligent than men, and yet the angels cannot fully comprehend the profound and deep secrets which are shut up in the council of the infinite trinity. David was an inspired man, but David said: "Such knowledge is too wonderful for me; it is high, I cannot attain to it."

To the devout Christian who believes the Bible, loves Jesus Christ and worships God in spirit and in truth, the mysteries connected with our holy religion are not an objection, but a fascination, always claiming reverential study and constantly increasing our spiritual comprehension of divine goodness and the glorious plan of human redemption.

The Apostle Paul beautifully reconciles us to present conditions when he writes in 1 Corinthians 13: 12, "For now we see through a glass darkly; but then face to face: now I know in part; but then shall I know even as also I am known."

Much of the destructive criticism of the times, which is producing widespread unbelief and contributing in a thousand ways to the increase of wickedness in the world, arises out of the fact that modern scholarship has produced among men an intellectual pride that scorns the simple faith of the devout child of God and purposes, by mere human philosophies, to solve all mysteries connected with the immaculate conception, the divine incarnation, the resurrection and the power of the sacrificial blood of the holy Christ to lift sinful men out of a state of degradation into a state of sanctification and oneness with the eternal Father.

There is nothing more marvelous in all the realm of revelation than the incarnation of Jesus Christ. The inspired writer says truly: " Without controversy great is the mystery of godliness: God was manifest in the flesh."

The rebellion and fall of man into a state of sinfulness brought so wide a separation between him and the infinitely holy God, the condition was so hopeless, the distance separating the two beings apart was so wide, the chasm so vast and deep, that in order to bridge it there must be brought into existence a mediator between God and man. Divine wisdom never rose to higher heights, or stooped to deeper depths of compassionate love than in the solving of the sin problem, rescuing man from his fallen condition and restoring him to a state of holiness and communion with his Maker. In accomplishing this great work, God found it necessary to offer a Redeemer so human that He could sympathize with man, and so divine that He could save man.

God had created men, but He had never been a man. God had seen men toil, but He had never blis-

tered His hands with carpenter's tools.  He had seen
men weep, but He had never wept.  He had seen men
struggling in the midst of temptation, but He had never
felt the onslaughts of the tempter against Himself.
He had seen men bleed, but He had never bled.  He
had seen the millions struggling on the crumbling
verge of the grave, and finally sinking into its hopeless
depths, but He had never felt the cold grip of death or
spread His omnipotent shoulders upon the bottom of
a sepulchre.  He determined, because it was a necessity in the discovery and opening up the way for a lost
and sinful race to return to purity, peace, and fellowship with Himself, to come into the world, to take the
weight of humanity upon Himself, to walk its rugged
paths, to carry its heavy burdens, to know its deep
sorrows and heart-breaking griefs, to meet and conquer
its tempter and destroyer, to suffer and die among its
outcasts and criminals, to lie down in the house of
death, and then to arise in majesty and rend the gate
of the tomb asunder, opening the way for a redeemed
race from the grace to the glorious resurrection and
eternal life.

The wisdom of the incarnation is seen when we
remember how difficult it is for the finite to grasp the
infinite, for the earthly to comprehend the heavenly,
for the sinful to approach the holy.  It is hard for us
to fix our thoughts upon that great Being without body
or parts, who is eternal in existence, omnipotent, and
omnipresent.  The poor human intellect staggers with
the thought.  We do not know where to begin, how to
proceed, or where to leave off.  The wings of our imagi-

nation grow weary, the brain grows dizzy, while the heart hungers on, and we are made to cry out in the language of Job: " Canst thou by searching find out God? Canst thou find out the Almighty unto perfection? It is as high as heaven; what canst thou do? deeper than hell; what canst thou know? The measure thereof is longer than the earth, and broader than the sea."

It is easy to think of the Babe of Bethlehem, and with the wise men to worship Him. Even in His infancy lying in a manger, He was a true object of worship. There is no intimation that the gathering of the eastern sages and the humble shepherds on bended knees about that wondrous Child was sacrilege. It is delightful to stand amidst priests and doctors of the law, listening to His wisdom while He is yet a youth; to go down to John's baptism and see Him standing meek and lowly in the presence of the rugged preacher and saying: " Suffer it to be so now, for thus it becometh us to fulfil all righteousness." It thrills us to follow Him up the mountain-side, to look with awe upon the temptation. The Second Adam has met with the foe before whom the first Adam fell, and we behold with joy the defeat of Satan, and the triumph of the world's Redeemer. We can trail Him along His pathway by the crutches and the canes which have been cast aside by the halt and lame He has healed, and the shouts and praises of those from whom devils have been cast out.

As we follow Him there is no doubt that He is God manifest in the flesh. He walks like a man, but He works like a God.  We behold His humanity when He lay sleeping in the boat, and His deity when He arises and rebukes the wind and storm, and the tempest sinks into silence at His command.  He weeps like a man at Lazarus' tomb, but with godlike voice He breaks the power of death and brings him forth alive.  As a man, He sits hungry at the well's mouth; like a God, He breaks the few loaves and little fishes and feeds the multitude.  Like a man, he goes into the mountains for prayer; like a God, He walks the waves of the Sea of Galilee and overtakes His disciples who have gone forth in the ship.  Like a man, He climbs the mountain; transfigured like a God, He stands upon its crest in garments whiter than the light.

What a marvelous combination of the two natures— human and divine!  Spirit begotten and virgin born. The eternal Spirit did not beget a *thing,* but a person. He did not beget an animal, but a man.  There is no teaching further from the tenor of the Holy Scriptures than that the visible Christ was some sort of strange creature, without human nature, mind or soul. Jesus had a human mind, which " grew in knowledge." He had a human soul, of which He said in Gethsemane, " My soul is exceeding sorrowful, even unto death."

In coming to the world's Redeemer, seeking to know something of Him and what He means to the world, and what He is to us, the Holy Scriptures weigh infinitely more with us than all the reasonings and philosophies of men.  They have absolute right-of-way. Turning to the Scriptures we find the inspired writer saying, " For verily he took not on him the nature of

angels; but he took on him the seed of Abraham."
That is, the nature of man. And again, "Wherefore
in all things it behooved him to be made like unto his
brethren, that he might be a merciful and faithful high
priest in things pertaining to God, to make reconcili-
ation for the sins of the people. For in that he himself
hath suffered being tempted, he is able to succor them
that are tempted."

J. G. Holland, in his sweetest poem, strikes the key-
note of the Gospel when he says: "Tempted in every
point like as ourselves was He tempted, yet without
sin. It was through temptation, thought I, that the
Lord, the Mediator between God and man, reached
down the sympathetic hand of love to meet the grasp
of lost humanity." It is through the knowledge of
this human kinship that men are enabled to approach,
trust in, and claim the mercy of Christ. It is through
His humanity that we approach the Son, and it is
through the Son that we come to the Father. Jesus
says, "No man cometh to the Father but by me."
"No man knoweth the Father, save the Son, and he to
whom the Son will reveal him."

It is by means of this divine Christ, who was made
like unto His brethren in body, mind, and soul, that
the wide chasm stretching between an infinitely holy
God and an utterly depraved and fallen man is
bridged; our Redeemer becomes to us a faithful "high
priest who can be touched with the feelings of our infirmities," and yet possessing in Himself that eternal
power and godhead which make Him one and equal
with the Father, able to save to the uttermost.

It is an inspiration to contemplate that great painting of Michael Angelo on the ceiling of the Sistine Chapel at Rome. In the picture he makes the Master to stand before the beholder " as the head of all humanity, as the goal of all progress, as the consummation of all glory." This picture has been called the most eloquent of all sermons on Christ's communion with the whole world. Standing in the presence of that picture, one's heart is thrilled as he contemplates the mysterious union of the two natures into one being, and seems to be looking upon the majesty and beauty of combined humanity and deity.

The conflict of the centuries has raged around Jesus Christ. He was unknown until He was manifest in the flesh, and the Father was unknown,—that is, He was never understood—until He was revealed in the Son. The world had heard of the eternal God. He had revealed Himself to a few men; the prophets had proclaimed His laws for our government, angels had now and again brought some message from the headquarters of the universe, but God was unknown until Jesus came, walked in our midst and communed with us. He sat down, ate with sinners, touched elbows with profane and wicked men, healed our sick, made our lame to leap for joy, our deaf to hear the tender melodies of His compassionate voice. He forgave those detected in the vilest sins, and everywhere and always lived on the highest planes of holiness and breathed the sweetest spirit of compassion and mercy.

When the disciples insisted that He should show them the Father, He said, " He that hath seen me hath seen the Father." What amazing words are these! We never could have had any such conception of the eternal God of the ages. We knew He could build a universe, fling the stars from His finger-tips into their orbits, but we never dreamed that He would become a carpenter and fix the windows in the hut of a poor man. We understood that He sat upon the throne of the universe and angels and archangels bowed in adoration at His feet, but it never occurred to us that He would sit down and partake of a frugal meal among sunburned fishermen. We understood that He commanded all the mighty hosts of heaven, that angels flew on lightning wing, that at His look and word devils fled in consternation, but we did not know that He would gather little children into His bosom and bless them with His caress and love.

Had Jesus not come to our earth, and lived with us here, had God not been manifest in the flesh, we never could have known the heart of the infinite Father. We are profoundly impressed, as never before, that there is closer kinship than we yet have dreamed between God and His creature, man, made in His image, redeemed by the incarnation and sufferings of His Son, adopted as His children, with the promise that we shall be satisfied when we awake in His likeness.

It seems to us that contemplation of these great facts in our holy religion ought to lead to a universal rebellion against sin,—a great heartcry for redemption from all of its effects, for restoration to purity of heart and holiness of life. The greatest need of our time is that we get away from mere theological theories and human philosophies about Christ and that we get back to Christ Himself. Not the Christ of men's notions, manufactured by this, that, and the other school of theology, but the Christ God gave to men; the Christ of the Gospels; the Christ of Bethlehem, Nazareth, Galilee, Bethany, Jerusalem, Gethsemane, Calvary, and Mt. Olivet; the Christ who lived and labored, hungered and suffered, loved and forgave; who died in tears and blood and agony on the Cross for a sinful race, arose in triumph over death.

The great Frederick W. Robertson, in his sermon on the sinlessness of Christ, makes this impressive statement: " There may be such an exclusive dwelling upon the divinity of Jesus as absolutely to destroy His real humanity; there may be such a morbid sensitiveness when we speak of Him as taking our nature, as will destroy the fact of His sufferings—yes, and destroy the reality of His atonement also. There is a way of speaking of the sinlessness of Jesus that would absolutely make that scene on Calvary a mere pageant, in which He was acting a part in a drama, during which He was not really suffering and did not really crush the propensities of His human nature."

Further on in the same sermon, he says: " Trust in divine humanity elevates the soul. It is done by hope. You must have observed the hopefulness of the character of Jesus—His hopefulness for human nature. If ever there were one who might have despaired, it was He. Full of love Himself, He was met with every sort of unkindness, every kind of derision. There was treachery in one of His disciples, dissension amongst

them all. He was engaged in the hardest work that
man ever tried. He was met by the hatred of the whole
world, by torture and the Cross; and yet never did the
hope of Human Nature forsake the Redeemer's soul.
He would not break the bruised reed, nor quench the
smoking flax. There was a spark mingling even in the
lowest Humanity, which He would fain have fanned
into a blaze. The lowest publican Jesus could call to
Him and touch his heart; the lowest profligate that was
ever trodden under foot by the world, was one for
whom He could hope still. If He met with penitents,
He would welcome them; if they were not penitents,
but yet felt the pangs of detected guilt, still with hopefulness he pointed to forgiven Humanity; this was His
word, even to the woman brought to Him by her ac-
cusers,—' Go and sin no more;' in His last moments
on the Cross, to one who was dying by His side, He
promised a place in Paradise: and the last words that
broke from the Redeemer's lips, what were they but
hope for our Humanity, while the curses were ringing
in His ears?—' Father, forgive them, for they know
not what they do.'"

We can no more permit the theologian and philos-
ophers to rob us of the humanity of Jesus, than we
can permit the destructive critic and skeptic to rob us
of the deity of Jesus. We must keep in our thought,
worship in our heart, and proclaim in our message to
the people the Christ of the Gospels, that human-divine
Being who lived, walked and talked with the disciples;
that human Christ who can be touched with the feelings of our infirmities; that divine Christ who is able

to save to the uttermost, who is the same yesterday, today and forever.

Henry van Dyke a few years ago delivered a lecture before the Divinity students of Yale University on the human life of God. This, with other lectures, he has bound up into a book entitled "The Gospel for an Age of Doubt." In the preface of this book, he says: "To seek Christ as the true Son of God, and the brother of all men, is to be sure that the soul is free, and that God is good, and that the end of life is noble service." In this lecture, to which we have referred, on the human life of God, van Dyke says: "This complete incarnation, this thorough trial under human conditions, this perfect discipline of obedience through suffering was a humiliation. But it was in no sense a degradation. On the contrary, it was a crowning of Christ with glory and honor in order that He might taste death for every man. 'For it became him, for whom are all things, and by whom are all things, in bringing many sons to glory, to make the Captain of their salvation perfect through suffering.' If the Epistle to the Hebrews teaches anything, it certainly teaches this. The humanity of Jesus was not the veiling but the unveiling of the divine glory. The limitations, temptations, and sufferings of manhood were the conditions under which alone Christ could accomplish the greatest work of the Deity—the redemption of a sinful race. The seat of the divine revelation and the center of the divine atonement was and is the human life of God."

The further we pursue our line of thought, the closer

we come to Jesus Christ, the more profoundly we are impressed with the text—" Great is the mystery of godliness." This beautiful Babe of Bethlehem, this wondrous youth of twelve years, this patient carpenter of Nazareth, this meek and lowly man followed by ignorant fishermen, " receiving sinners and eating with them," this matchless preacher of the truth, this majestic Master of devils, disease and death; this man in bloody sweat in Gethsemane, this victim of human hate and mob violence falling beneath His burden on Calvary's hillside, this white-faced, sinless Jesus hanging on the Cross—Do you know who he is! He is God manifest in the flesh.

Do you ask what all of this means! It means that the good Shepherd of heaven has come to earth seeking His lost sheep. It means the redemption of sinners; it means that fallen men are to be born again and become in Christ new creatures. It means that the depraved and sinful are to become sanctified, that strangers to the commonwealth of Israel are to become the sons of God. It means that the demon-possessed are to sit clothed and in their right minds at the Master's feet. It means that this man of Galilee, this Jesus of Nazareth is God manifest in the flesh to save a lost race; that sinful men are to partake of the divine nature, that the demon-possessed on their way to hell are to become pure and holy beings, are to walk in righteousness through the earth and to ascend in triumph to heaven. Wondrous Christ, mighty to save!

Jesus Christ belonged to no special race of men. He was the Son of man, the own full brother of every man of every race.  His kinship with men helps us to love and hope for all men.  He belonged to no special age. He belonged to all ages, to all time, to all eternity.  He was with the Father before the world was.  Abraham saw His day and was glad.  Moses promises his coming.  Micah tells us that He was to be born in Bethlehem.  David sings of Him in a hundred Psalms, Isaiah describes His humble person, His patient suffering, His cruel death, and His final triumph.

The eternal God, in the person of His Son, got off the throne of the universe, came down into a wicked world, was born in a stable, lay in a manger, grew up in poverty, lived amid hardships, labored with His hands and suffered for the necessaries of life.  After the day of toil He had not where to lay His head.  He conquered Satan.  He overcame the prejudices of men. The wife of Pilate sent him a message, saying, " Have nothing to do with this just man."  Pilate said, " I find in him no fault at all."  Judas Iscariot confessed, " I have betrayed innocent blood."  The captain of the band who crucified Him on the Cross said, " Certainly this was a righteous man."

The civilized world today acknowledges Him the Son of God.  The heathen world begs to hear His Gospel.  The multitudes of earth ask to be baptized in His name and millions of redeemed souls are waiting with hope and prayer for His coming.  We believe in Him, we worship Him, we pledge and consecrate our all to Him.  We cry to the lost race—" Behold the Lamb of God, which taketh away the sin of the world."

## II

## THE SECOND COMING OF CHRIST

*" That thou keep this commandment without spot, unrebuke-
able, until the appearing of our Lord Jesus Christ: which in his
times he shall show, who is the blessed and only Potentate, the
King of kings and Lord of lords."*—1 TIMOTHY 6: 14, 15.

ST. PAUL fully appreciated the fact that when
our Lord Jesus appears in His glory all debate
with reference to His Godhead, His power to
save, and the honor and worship which are His due,
will come to an abrupt and eternal end. The resurrection of Jesus Christ fully confirmed the faith of the
apostles in His Godhead. It was a final and complete
witness to His mastery over death, the last enemy.
Their doubts all vanished; their questions were all an-
swered. His resurrection was a final and sufficient
credential of His deity, of His authority, of the trustworthiness of all His promises, and the power of His
gospel to save a lost world.

When Jesus appears with the holy angels in His
glory in the heavens, His enemies shall be put to utter
rout. That will be a final, positive proof of His pre-
existence, His Virgin Birth, the fact of His miracles, of
His resurrection, of His eternal Godhead, and right to
reign and rule " King of kings and Lord of lords."
We can think of nothing,—in fact there could be
nothing—that would more completely overthrow and

scatter forever all of the foes and opposers of our Master, the Lord Jesus Christ, than that He should appear, as foretold by Himself and by the apostolic writers.

It will be recalled that when Jesus stood before the high priests with the scribes and elders after His arrest on that tragic night in the Garden of Gethsemane, and the high priest said to Him, " I adjure thee by the living God, that thou tell us whether thou be the Christ, the Son of God." " Jesus saith unto him, Thou hast said: nevertheless I say unto you, hereafter shall ye see the Son of man sitting on the right hand of power, and coming in the clouds of heaven."

Jesus was giving the high priest, the scribes and the elders, faithful warning that they might do their worst, but after their worst was done, the time was coming when He would appear in His glory and they would be compelled to admit His deity and divine Sonship.

The Jews living during the period of our Lord's ministry among men failed to get any sort of proper conception of Christ's person and mission in the world. To the ordinary student of the Holy Scriptures, it seems quite remarkable that these Jews should have so misunderstood, hated, and persecuted the Lord Jesus. To us, it seems that His personality, teachings, and life fitted so perfectly into the prophecies concerning Him that any one at all acquainted with those prophecies would have identified Him as the Messiah. How was it that the Jews failed to recognize Jesus of Nazareth as the Christ of prophecy?

First, they were in a fearful state of spiritual apostasy and blindness, and spiritual things are spiritually discerned.  Second, they did not understand that it was the plan of God that Christ, in accomplishing the great task assigned to Him, was to come twice into the world. No one in ancient or modern times can correctly interpret the prophecies concerning the Christ who does not recognize this fact.

If we would get at anything approaching a correct and satisfactory comprehension of the true meaning of prophecy concerning Jesus Christ, we must divide these prophecies into at least two general groups. First, there is a group of prophecies that foretell Christ's coming, sufferings, humiliation and death, with the inauguration of the Gospel dispensation. Second, there is another group of prophecies that tell of Christ's coming in power to set up His kingdom and reign over His redeemed people, clearly indicating the glory and power of that kingdom and reign.

The Jews failed to understand this important fact and, as a consequence, could not rightly divide and properly group the prophecies concerning Christ. Eventually, they lost sight of all those prophecies foretelling the humiliation and sufferings of Jesus which must occur at His first coming, and fixed their minds only upon those prophecies which pointed to the restoration of Israel, the overthrow of their enemies and the triumphant rule and reign of their Messiah. They unwittingly cut out the Gospel, or Church Age, and put the Kingdom Age in its place.  They had so misread the predictions and promises of the prophets that they were not looking for a Redeemer from sin to set up a kingdom of righteousness, peace and joy in the hearts of men. In their spiritual blindness they had no conception of, or desire for, a Redeemer from their sins. They were not hoping and praying for spiritual salvation. They wanted political deliverance and national glory. They were not looking for an Evangel preaching righteousness, but for a King breaking the yoke of Rome. Their minds were fixed on Scriptures found in Isaiah: " Behold, a king shall reign in righteousness, and princes shall rule in judgment. And a man shall be as a hiding place from the wind, and a covert from the tempest; as rivers of water in a dry place, as the shadow of a great rock in a weary land " (Isaiah 32: 1, 2). Jeremiah had said, " And I will set up shepherds over them which shall feed them; and they shall fear no more, nor be dismayed, neither shall they be lacking, saith the Lord. Behold the days come, saith the Lord, that I will raise unto David a righteous Branch, and a King shall reign and prosper, and shall execute judgment and justice in the earth. In his days Judah shall be saved, and Israel shall dwell safely " (Jer. 23: 4, 5). Daniel had given them a wonderful prophecy: " And in the days of these kings shall the God of heaven set up a kingdom, which shall never be destroyed; and the kingdom shall not be left to other people, but it shall break in pieces and consume all these kingdoms, and it shall stand forever " (Daniel 2: 44).

Many prophecies of this character might be quoted with which the Jews were perfectly familiar, and upon which they rested their hope for a coming Messiah and king to deliver them from their enemies and avenge them upon all those nations which had despoiled them. It never occurred to the Jews that while all these Scriptures were absolutely true, and had reference to the humble Nazarene standing in their midst, that the fulfillment of these promises belonged to a future dispensation in the history of the world and at a time far removed from that in which they were living. They were blinded by ambition and prejudice.

When the meek and lowly Christ appeared among them claiming to be the long-promised Messiah, they could see nothing in Him that met their conception of their coming king. They were disgusted and angered with His claims and with the rebukes He administered to them. They were startled as they saw the influence He had over the masses of the people, and determined to put Him to death for fear that His followers would inaugurate a revolt against the authority of Rome, which they were quite sure would lead to severe vengeance and a more tyrannical administration of Roman authority.

They hated Jesus on general principles, and determined to take His life under the pretext of political necessity. In their blindness they had no conception of what they were doing. While suffering on the Cross our Lord looked down upon the jeering mob and prayed, " Father, forgive them; they know not what they do." What few spiritual Jews were then living recognized Jesus as the Messiah. Simeon knew Him; Anna, the aged saint, recognized Him. Joseph and Nicodemus knew that He was a man come from

God, but the proud ecclesiastics and the dupes under their control, could not possibly understand the Christ or the prophecies concerning Him, because they did not understand that in the great scheme of human salvation, and the restoration of all things, it was the plan of God that Christ must come *twice* into the world; the first time, He was to make His advent through the open door of a stable; the second time He was to make His advent through the open heaven. The first time He was to come in great humiliation; the second time He was to come in great glory. The first time He was to ride into Jerusalem on an ass's colt; the second time He was to ride into Jerusalem on the shekinah cloud. At His first coming, He was to hang upon the Cross amidst the derision of the multitude; at His second coming He was to sit upon the throne of universal empire and reign over His redeemed peoples.

The Jews had so misread prophecy that they got their program at least two thousand years ahead of God's plan. Hence, their inability to understand what was transpiring before them. They wanted to place the Messiah on the throne when, according to the divine purpose, He was due on the Cross. There are some Christians, who misreading prophecy, are as completely out of harmony with the divine program as were the Jews. There are Christians who would keep Christ on the Cross when He is almost due on the throne. The Jews wanted to crown a king when they ought to have been worshipping the Babe of Bethlehem. There is a class of Christians who insist on lingering about Bethlehem when they ought to be preparing to shout Hosannas to the coming King. The Jews who failed to rightly divide prophecy did not want a Redeemer from sin; they wanted to set up a universal empire in the world. There is a class of Christians who do not want to crown Christ King of kings and Lord of lords to rule the world in peace and blessedness. They want to set up a great world-wide ecclesiasticism. Not long since, one of the leaders of that group of professed Christians who would have the Lord delay His coming said, with startled disgust, " Why, if Jesus should come now it would interfere with our program." He seemed to think that God has no program. He admitted at once that he and those who sympathized with him had a program, but it entirely left out the glorious appearing of our blessed Lord.

The destructive critics can no more understand the program of God as revealed in prophecy and taught by the Lord Jesus and His disciples, which embraces both His first and His second coming, than those ancient Jews who crucified our Lord, and in their blindness they are " crucifying the Son of God afresh." Being spiritually blind, they cannot rightly divide the word of truth, and they are no more ready to crown Jesus at His second coming than the ancient Jews were to recognize and trust in Him as their Messiah and Saviour at His first coming.

The Christian Church, although it has accomplished great good in the world, has largely failed in her mission to preach the Gospel to every creature, because she has failed to understand the Word of God, and the plainly written predictions of the prophets and promises of Christ and the apostles with reference to His second appearing in glory. Having failed to understand the program of God, they have made many programs of their own which conflict with the divine plan and fail to accomplish the divine purpose. Hence, almost two thousand years after the death of our Redeemer, untold millions of people are living in midnight darkness in the midst of sin, disease, starvation and death because they have not had brought to them the glorious Gospel message of the Lord Jesus.

The program of Christ was that He should come into the world meek and lowly, to live before men, to teach them the way of salvation, to die for them and to set on foot an aggresive evangelism, to make haste in carrying the Gospel to all the world. While this evangelism was going forward He was to go and prepare a place for His people. When the Gospel had been preached to all the world for witness, He was to return in clouds of glory and catch away His Bride— the Church. Then the wicked multitudes who had rejected the Gospel would bring upon themselves the " great tribulations;" a time of destruction would prevail in the world, not necessarily God-sent, but wicked men who had denied the pre-existence of Jesus, His Virgin Birth, His blood atonement and His second coming, having flung away the Bible and plunged into the black night of an awful infidelity, reaping the harvest that eventually must spring up and grow from the seed now being sown by the destructive critics. Thus men will bring upon themselves swift destruction.

They are doing it now.  They reached a fearful climax during the World War, but they are preparing for a darker day.  Finally, Christ will return with the bride which He has caught away, and bring order out of chaos, peace out of war, and then those prophecies and promises so glorious in the Holy Scriptures shall be fulfilled, and the kingdoms of this world shall become the kingdoms of our Lord and His Christ, and the knowledge of the glory of the Lord shall cover the earth as the waters cover the sea.

Had the Church properly interpreted prophecy, had she seen that Christ, in harmony with the divine program, was coming twice into the world, the first time to suffer and die and to set on foot a Gospel Dispensation, to speedily offer repentance and salvation to the entire human race, and then to come again in glory and power to overthrow wickedness and reign in righteousness over those who had accepted Him, what a different history she would have had.

With what remarkable zeal the disciples who saw and understood the great truth of our Lord's return carried forward the Gospel program.  How rapidly, without railroads, steamships, automobiles, or any of the modern methods of rapid transit, they carried the Gospel to the various nations and people of their time. How quickly the churches of today with their untold millions of money, methods of travel, printing press, wireless telegraphy and the close touch with the ends of the earth could carry the Gospel to every creature if she could once grasp the great truth that the mission of Jesus Christ in the world was not to set up great ecclesiasticisms, but to set on foot a great evangelism; not to build up sectarian prejudices among men, but to offer a Gospel which has in it power to save men from sin, and to realize that her highest mission is to proclaim this Gospel to every being beneath the sun.

There is not a hint in the teachings of Christ or His inspired apostles that during the Gospel Dispensation the entire population of the earth would be brought to repentance, saving faith and into harmony with God and peace among men. It is the duty of the Church to give every one an opportunity; to impress upon every one the privilege and the necessity of receiving Christ; always and everywhere, there has been and will be those who will reject the Gospel. The Church is not responsible for those who reject, but it is her duty to give the Gospel to all men.

The Scriptures teach us that there will be opposition. Jesus said to His disciples, " Behold I send you forth as sheep among wolves." He promised them crosses, reproaches, self-sacrifice and suffering, but in the midst of all this they were to have spiritual victory. He said to them, " In the world ye shall have tribulation: but be of good cheer; I have overcome the world." In the parable of the tares and the wheat we are taught that this dispensation is to be one of mixed good and evil, and will be so until the harvest time when the separation shall take place.

Jesus teaches us that at His coming to catch away His bride, many will be unprepared. In the parable of the wise and foolish virgins this truth is brought out very clearly. We find one-half of those who were awaiting the Bridegroom were unprepared to go with Him into the wedding feast. They lacked one essential—they had no oil. They had the form of godliness without the power.

If the preaching of the gospel is to bring in a millennium of perfection and glory and all are to be saved, and if at the end of this golden age Jesus comes, how is it that this parable teaches that when He does come, a large per cent of those who are expecting His coming will be unprepared to meet Him? If the post-millennial teaching be true the parable of the wise and foolish virgins is incapable of intelligent interpretation.

The post-millennial teaching of the Lord's coming no more harmonizes with the teachings of the New Testament than the Jewish notion of the Messiah's appearing as a king at His first coming harmonizes with the Old Testament teaching concerning the Messiah. Let us with reverence inquire of our Lord about this matter. Gracious Master, will the preaching of the Gospel finally bring the world—everybody upon the earth—into a saved state and ready to meet Thee at Thy coming? The answer of Jesus is:

" For nation shall rise against nation, and kingdom against kingdom: and there shall be famines, and pestilences, and earthquakes, in divers places. All these are the beginning of sorrows. Then shall they deliver you up to be afflicted, and shall kill you: and ye shall be hated of all nations for my name's sake. And then shall many be offended, and shall betray one another, and shall hate one another. And many false prophets shall arise, and shall deceive many. And because iniquity shall abound, the love of many shall wax cold. But he that shall endure unto the end, the same shall be saved. And this gospel of the kingdom shall be preached in all the world for a witness unto all nations; and then shall the end come " (Matt. 24: 7-14).

Lord, some people think there will be a millennium for a thousand years of warless peace and happiness on the earth just before Thy coming. Please tell us about this. Jesus says:

" Immediately after the tribulation of those days shall the sun be darkened, and the moon shall not give her light, and the stars shall fall from heaven, and the powers of the heavens shall be shaken; and then shall appear the sign of the Son of man in heaven: and then shall all the tribes of the earth mourn, and they shall see the Son of man coming in the clouds of heaven with power and great glory. And he shall send his angels with a great sound of a trumpet, and they shall gather together his elect from the four winds, and from one end of heaven to the other. Now learn a parable of the fig tree; when his branch is yet tender, and putteth forth leaves, ye know that summer is nigh; so likewise ye, when ye shall see all these things, know that it is near, even at the doors " (Matt. 24: 29-33).

But, Lord, will not the preachers so know and explain Thy word to the people that they will all understand the divine plan, and be expecting Thee, and ready to receive Thee, joyfully, at Thy coming? Christ answers:

" For as in the days that were before the flood, they were eating and drinking, marrying and giving in mar-

riage, until the day that Noah entered into the ark.
And knew not until the flood came, and took them all
away; so shall also the coming of the Son of man be.
Then shall two be in the field; the one shall be taken,
and the other left. Two women shall be grinding at
the mill; the one shall be taken, and the other left.
Watch therefore: for ye know not what hour your Lord
doth come " (Matt. 24: 38-42).

What are we to think of men in the light of these
words of Jesus Christ, who persist in telling us that
our Lord delayeth His coming for twenty, fifty, or
perhaps a hundred thousand years, and that the eccle-
siastical forces in the world will bring all men into a
state of perfect peace and righteousness before the
Lord comes? Many of them assure us that He will
not come at all. We have boastful men in the Church
who tell us that Jesus believed He was coming back,
but that He was *mistaken*. Meanwhile we have repre-
sentatives of the Church who are cutting the Bible to
pieces, denying the Virgin Birth and Deity of our
Lord, excusing sin and denying the existence of the
devil, or a place of future punishment. In the World
War, almost all white soldiers had been baptized in the
name of Jesus Christ. They were Roman Catholics in
southern Europe, they were Greek Catholics in north-
ern Europe, the English-speaking soldiers, a large per
cent of them, had been baptized in their infancy, many
others had been baptized of their own free will, and
yet these great masses of church members fighting and
killing each other, with their religious teachers and
leaders, knew but little more of the great plan of God,

—the real Gospel and the mission of Christ to save men from sin, and His second coming to reign over them, than did the Jews who lived on the earth at the time of Christ's ministry among men.

We are by no means saying that the Gospel has not accomplished much, but we are saying it has not been preached at all to untold millions of men, and that it has not been taught properly to vast multitudes who have heard it. Had the German Kaiser, the Russian Czar, the King of Italy, the President of France, the king of Austria and the King of England been earnest pre-millennial Christians, " loving the Lord's appearing," the World War would have been an impossibility. Men have forgotten that God has a program, that Jesus Christ is a King, and that He is coming to rule. In their blindness and ignorance of the Word of God, the will and plans of God, and the true character of the Son of God, they go about to set up their own kingdoms and have their own way. The results—war, bloodshed, death and desolation.

Our only hope for universal peace and a warless age is the coming of Christ and His Kingdom. Then, and not until then, will a true brotherhood be established among men of all nations, kindreds, tongues and tribes.

Let us ask St. Paul with reference to the condition of things when our Lord shall appear. Paul, what will be the state of society and world conditions when Jesus comes? " For when they shall say, peace and safety; then sudden destruction cometh upon them, as travail upon a woman with child, and they shall not escape. But ye, brethren, are not in darkness, that that day should overtake you as a thief. Ye are all the children of light, and the children of the day: we are not of the night, nor of darkness. Therefore let us not sleep, as do others; but let us watch and be sober."

Notice the Apostle: " Let us not sleep, as do others." The Scripture plainly teaches that the coming of the Lord shall find some in spiritual sleep, unpreparedness; that His coming will be to some " sudden destruction." This is the whole tenor of the teaching of Paul. He prophesies that in the last days perilous times shall come; that men will be selfish, lovers of pleasure rather than lovers of God; that they will seek for false teachers; that they will give heed to doctrines of devils; that many will have their consciences seared as with a hot iron.

Beloved, can we read these prophecies of the Apostle, compare them with the teachings of Jesus, look upon the signs of the times about us and remain indifferent, follow after pleasure, seek to lay up useless treasures in this world, sit in silence and indifference to the false teachings and the vast number of people who are being deceived and led away from the saving Gospel? Must we not arouse ourselves and do everything in our power to bring the people to repentance and saving faith in Jesus; to spread the Gospel to all the world, to bring to the heathen who have so long sat in darkness the good news of salvation, and to keep our own spiritual lamps trimmed and burning, and our vessels filled with oil that we may be ready to meet the Bridegroom at His coming?

# III

## THE MODERN JUDAS

*"And he cast down the pieces of silver in the temple, and departed, and went and hanged himself."*—MATTHEW 27: 5.

WE have recorded here the last acts of that unfortunate fellow-being, Judas Iscariot, who sold his Master for thirty pieces of silver, betrayed Him with a kiss, and made himself to be regarded as the monster criminal of all ages. I suppose there is no name in the history of mankind that carries a greater weight of human contempt than that of Judas Iscariot. Robert Ingersoll was an infidel; he denied the inspiration of the Scriptures, the deity of the Lord Jesus, and mocked at our holy Christianity. He had several sons, but he took pains not to name one of them Judas Iscariot.

There can be no question but what Judas Iscariot is a lost man. He drifted away from Christ, he fell into the snare of Satan, committed a fearful crime, played the hypocrite, committed suicide, and the inspired writer tells us, " he went to his own place." There are no reasonable grounds for hope that Judas Iscariot is a saved man. Somewhere in the dark prison-house of lost souls, with the memory of his crime burning like fire into his consciousness, he wanders desolate, lost and doomed forever. If my saying so made it so, I

38

would not utter these words; but I say it because it is so. It ought to be a warning. Men who live in sin and die in sin go out into certain and awful doom.

I have never been able to understand how a minister of the Gospel, with all the facts in the case before him, could stand up in the pulpit and try to make out a good case for Judas Iscariot. Our Lord Jesus gave as an epitaph to write upon the tombstone of this unfortunate man: " It had been good for that man if he had not been born." Jesus could not have said this of a man who was going to spend an eternity in Heaven. However sinful a man might be, however criminal, however far he may have wandered from God, if he repents, is pardoned and saved in Heaven for all eternity, it is fortunate for him that he was born. Jesus says it had been better for Judas that he had not been born. Judas Iscariot is a lost soul. It's a solemn thought that a man who knew the Lord Jesus, who evidently believed the Old Testament Scriptures, who was called into the discipleship, who heard the parables, beheld the miracles, and had the marvelous privileges and advantages with which Judas Iscariot was surrounded, should have gone away into sin, and gone out into darkness. We shall meditate for awhile upon this man's conduct and character and find, if we can, the cause of the lapse of his faith, his drifting away into wickedness, and his final plunge into the deepest depths of apostasy and sin.

We are told in the inspired record that Judas was the treasurer for the little group of disciples. " He carried the bag and kept that which was put therein."

The handling of money seems to be dangerous. Men grow to love money; the clink of it becomes the sweetest of music to their ears, and the engravings on it become to them the highest art. They would turn away from the most splendid symphonies to listen to the jingle of gold; they would hurry out of the greatest art galleries to look with admiration upon the engravings on the coin which is becoming their god, the chief desire of their souls, the object of their worship.

Handling the money and counting it, Judas came to love it, and began to appropriate it. Nothing can be more degrading than for a man to betray the trust of his friends; while he smiles and holds up his head as if he were honest, he filches from those who trust him with their substance. The least deviation from honesty is a most dangerous sin; it springs a leak in the bottom of a man's moral boat, and by and by it will submerge him in wreck and ruin. Sins are very sociable; they are rarely bachelors. They become married to vice and have large families. One sin calls for another. If a man steals he will lie, and of course hypocrisy comes along. By and by the thief and liar will commit murder in order to escape detection. Such a man will break the Sabbath and, if opportunity offers, he will be unclean in his life. Opportunity need not offer; he will seek opportunity for any sin.

It seems that Judas got to love money so well, and became so interested in it, he had little time for anything else. I have an idea that the working of miracles became a very commonplace thing with him. He would hardly notice the healing of the sick or the raising of the dead. His mind was pre-occupied. He might have stood very near to Jesus while He preached to the multitudes, and scarcely heard what He said; he was absorbed. He had come to love money and was planning for collections. The more he got into his hands the more economical he would become in bearing the expenses of the group, and the more he could appropriate for his own personal use. Poor Judas! Let no one suppose that he is the only man that ever trod this slippery path that leads so certainly to the brink of ruin.

The love of money mastered Judas. It crowded the love of Christ out of him. His faith in money, that it could make him happy, that the possession of it was the chief end of man, crowded faith in Jesus Christ out of his heart. He found that the teaching of Jesus *was* true and *is* true: "No man can serve two masters." Judas, absorbed in money-getting, losing his faith in, and his love for, the Master, was full of indignation when a devoted woman in the joy of her love, broke an alabaster box of precious ointment and poured the entire contents upon our beloved Lord and Saviour. He looked with hatred upon the woman, and with displeasure upon the Lord Jesus that he should have permitted such a waste of money in so extravagant an anointing. What malice, what hypocrisy, as his eyes glared and his anger burned within him, as he hissed out of his wicked lips: "Why was this waste of the ointment made? It might have been sold for much and given to the poor." "Not that he cared for the poor," says the inspired record, "but he was a thief

and carried the bag and kept what was put therein."
Poor Judas!

We find in further reading that Satan put it into his
heart to betray Christ; and still further, we find the
startling statement that " Satan entered into him." So
we see this man going constantly from bad to worse.
When Satan can put things into a man he can soon
enter into the place where he has been storing up purposes, desires, and evil intentions and, having entered
into a man, he dominates him; he can drive him to any
crime; he can force him to take his own life; he can
make him to hurry himself into the hot pits of torment.

It will be remembered that Judas maintained his
pretense of devotion to the very end. He had prac-
ticed deception until he had become an expert in his
hypocrisy. You will recall that when he got his thirty
pieces of silver and secured the company of soldiers he
said to his miserable associates: " Whomsoever I shall
kiss, that same is he." And as they are starting out
for their diabolical purpose he is heard to say, " Hold
Him fast." He evidently wanted them to understand,
" If He gets away from you, don't blame me with it;
don't come back on me for the thirty pieces; He's
yours; this is mine; I'll keep this whatever may become
of your plans." Poor Judas! His blasted, devil-
possessed soul hadn't left in it a shred of faith or a
mite of love. He was money-mastered; the passion for
silver had burned out all devotion and left his soul a
charred cinder.

The effect of sin upon a human soul is something
fearful to contemplate. And perhaps there is no sin so

blighting, which sits upon a nest full of the eggs of evil and hatches out so horrible a brood of wickedness, as the love of money. It can eat as doth a canker. It can sully and soil the whitest souls into the blackness of midnight. It can lead on at a gallop to the most horrible crimes. Now that Judas had his money he has a bit of time to think. There is no business pressing him at the moment; he has accomplished his task and he can pause for a little while in his business enterprises and look over the situation. He attends the trial; he hears the testimony; he sees the mob spit in the face of Jesus; he hears the whistle of the lash; he sees the oozing blood; he has an awakening. The slumbering volcano within him begins to tremble, the smoke rises, and the red fires of his torment begin to lick out their wrathful tongues. He loses his love for money. He doesn't want houses, land, food, or clothing. His soul has awakened. It is like a raving wild beast; it tears him with awful torture. The only thing he desires is a rope and some place to tie one end of it; he intends his miserable neck for the other end.

Judas has kindled a fire within his own breast which blazes up into an unendurable torment. He cannot endure himself. St. Paul reaches a climax of testimony when he says, " For me to live is Christ." His life was lost, surrendered and swallowed up in his Redeemer and Lord. For Judas to live was torment; torment he could not endure, and he took the plunge of the suicide, but he found that the destruction of his body brought him no relief. His suffering was not physical; it was not his body which was tormenting him; it was the soul. It was in a horror of remorse and despair. The man who commits suicide, supposing that he can get away from spiritual and mental agony, makes a great mistake. If his agonizing soul remained in the body he might be able to seek and find salvation, but when he turns that soul out by destroying his physical life, it is undone, without hope or possibility of salvation. Death offers no remedy to the agony of a sinful soul. The suicides leave behind their poor, poisoned, stabbed or drowned bodies, but they have not gotten rid of the torture that drove them to suicide. Judas found that he could not kill himself; he could not get away from his personality, nor escape from the fiery torture of a sin-blighted spirit.

What was the matter with Judas Iscariot? He loved thirty pieces of silver better than he loved Jesus. What is the matter with any sinner? He loves something better than he loves Christ. That thing, whatever it may be, that comes between him and the Saviour of men, that keeps him from accepting Christ as his Saviour, as certainly proves his ruin as the thirty pieces of silver proved the ruin of Judas Iscariot.

May I ask, Is Jesus on the market today? Is anybody selling Christ? It seems to me there is but one correct answer. Many deluded souls have put Christ on the market. Here is a man, for instance, who is receiving five, seven, or ten thousand dollars a year to stand up before an unregenerated and wealthy congregation of people and sell Christ. He tells them that Jesus is not of Virgin Birth, that He is not God manifest in the flesh; that His death was unnecessary; that

He never performed any miracles; that He made no atonement for sin in His death. Isn't this selling Christ? He may perform his work more adroitly, and no doubt receives a larger price for his horrible deed, but isn't he worse than Judas Iscariot? Hasn't he more light than Judas had? Isn't he selling the Christ out of the church, out of the creed, out of the faith and love of the people? Won't his conduct bring untold numbers into doubt and finally into doom?

The modern Judas can peddle Jesus out very gracefully. He uses beautiful language; he makes claim to great scholarship; he insists that he is deeply pious. He has practically gotten above law, and cares nothing for doctrine. Such things are entirely too material for him. He is a kind of orchid; his roots are not buried in the common soil of Bible teaching, but they are reaching out into pure nothingness. He is unlike Judas in one particular; he doesn't hang himself. He has gotten his conscience in a condition where he can betray the Lord, see Him laughed at, His Virgin Birth denied, the atoning merit of His death denied, and the lash of criticism and ridicule laid upon the Christ. He has sold the Lord, but he makes no inquiry for a rope. He goes on putting Jesus on the market and peddling Him out to the congregation that is the highest bidder.

Sometimes the modern Judas is found in the chair of a religious institution. He is tearing up the Old Testament and putting his scissors into the New Testament. Jesus quoted from, and approved, Moses, but the modern Judas makes Jesus an ignorant teacher, putting His endorsement upon writing which Moses

never wrote. He has a blend of sympathy and ridicule
for the poor Nazarene who lived entirely too early in
the history of the world to know the facts with reference to the writing of this ancient literature called the
Bible. He sells our Lord without a qualm of conscience. He sleeps soundly and fattens on the price
he receives for the skepticism he peddles, the Christ
he belittles and the market he makes of the world's
Redeemer.

We fear many men are making merchandise of the
Christ and the Gospel of Christ who little suspect
themselves to be possessed of the Judas spirit. It is a
fearful thing for a man to seek to enrich himself with
an emasculated Gospel by pretending to preach the
truth when he is amusing and pleasing sinners and
receiving their liberal contributions instead of warning, rebuking and winning their souls. It is a dangerous thing to take selfishness into the pulpit, or to in
any way make merchandise of our Lord.

Suppose a man should go around collecting money
for an institution. He is a skeptic, doesn't believe the
Old Testament, and has many criticisms for much of
the New. His sympathies are all with the liberals, but
he is among an orthodox and devout people. He desires his thirty pieces, his thirty thousand, or it may
be his million. It will never do for him to reveal his
real self. He must please the audience; he must fling
his hands up into the air and exhort. He must insist
that there is no hope for the world apart from the
Gospel. He must say that Jesus and Jesus alone, can
lift the mired wheel of humanity out of the rut and

apart from Him there is no help for these troublous times. He is after money and is playing a part. If he were with his own crowd, he would deny the blood atonement, and deny the resurrection. Wasn't all that noise and pretext of his, when in the presence of God's people, from whom he was seeking money to advance his unchristian propaganda, a mere Judas kiss? Wasn't he saying, " Hail, Master! " with a purpose of deceiving his Lord and the disciples of his Lord? Without doubt, he was. In what respect is the modern Judas any better man, any truer Christian, than the original Judas?

I fear that many men and women are putting Christ on the market. They are imagining themselves to be shrewd and successful money-gatherers and manipulators of the Kingdom of God, when they are only peddling Jesus around for whatever they can get for Him. There will come an awakening. There will come a time when they can deceive their souls no longer; when the fire will break out and their souls will become a furnace of agony. Poor deluded and miserable creatures! They are laughing now; they are boasting that they are in the saddle; they congratulate themselves that they hold the positions of power and influence. What will they do when our Lord appears? What excuse can they make, to whom can they turn? They may cry to the rocks and mountains to fall on them, but they will find there is no ocean deep enough to engulf their guilt, no mountain tall enough to bury them out of the sight of Him who through the years they have been selling for silver, for

applause, for place, for influence and now and then
with their compliments have been playing the part of
Judas who betrayed his Master with a kiss.  Judgment Day is coming.  It will be an hour of uncover-
ing; a day of doom to those who have torn the Bible
into tatters and put Jesus Christ on the market and
sold Him for their mess of pottage, or for their millions of yellow gold which will turn to burning
brimstone.

Nothing can be more dangerous than trying to use
Jesus Christ with a selfish motive.  Not long since a
prominent ecclesiastic on his deathbed said to a friend,
" My soul is now in torment.  My agonies cannot be
described in words.  I have sold Jesus.  I have not
sought to elevate Him, but I have sought to use Him,
His Gospel, His Church, His influence in order to elevate myself.  The long years of my ministry have been
utterly selfish.  I am groping in darkness.  I am going
into eternal night."  And so he died.  How careful
the pastor should be to see that he is not seeking ap-
proval, popularity and salary from his people, but he
is lifting up and magnifying Jesus Christ and seeking
to bring his people into a state of salvation and devoted service.

How careful the evangelist should be not to set his
heart upon a large collection, but upon a gracious revival, to forget himself and the mere dollars and cents
feature of his meeting, and lift up Jesus to the admiration of the people; to forget the money in their pockets
in his great desire for the salvation of their souls.

It must be distinctly understood that Jesus Christ

must have the first place, not only in the hearts of ministers of the Gospel, but in all of His disciples. There are no circumstances under which Jesus Christ can consent to take second place. He must be Lord of all.

# IV

## THE VICTORY OF FAITH

*" If thou canst believe, all things are possible to him that believeth."*—MARK 9: 23.

THE statement contained in this text, "All things are possible," is so comprehensive in its scope that we would be tempted to question its trustworthiness but for one fact: it was, and is, the word of our Lord Jesus Christ. When He speaks, we ask no questions and offer no objection. Jesus Christ is the source, center, and fountain-head of all truth, authority, and power. We seek to understand properly and interpret the true meaning of His words, but we are ever ready to accept them at their full value. In the study of this text, we find there are certain qualifications and limitations with reference to the possibility of "*all things.*" Let us notice them:

The incident which brought forth the declaration, "All things are possible," is quite familiar. It was directly after the beautiful mystery of the transfiguration upon the mountain-top, where our Lord, in the presence of certain chosen disciples, was made to shine forth in His glory, and was visited by Moses and Elias and conversed with them. This was one of the most remarkable events in all the earthly life of the Lord Jesus. It was at this time that the three disciples present heard the voice of God out of the cloud saying, "This is my beloved son; hear ye him."

Now, it was directly after this wonderful display of His glory and this gracious endorsement of the Eternal Father that Jesus declared "all things are possible." You recall that when He came down from the mountain, He found the multitude gathered about His disciples with a man who had brought his sadly afflicted son who was possessed with an evil spirit. It seems the disciples had tried to cast out this spirit, but had failed, and the father made a most earnest plea to our Lord for help. The son was in no condition to have faith for himself; evidently, his mental faculties and moral perception were in no condition to lay hold upon Christ for deliverance. Some one must exercise faith for him. Just here is a gleam of light on an important subject, that of believing for others. There seems to be but one obstacle that can stand in the way of the mighty works of Christ; that one obstacle is unbelief. He could turn water into wine; He could command the storm-swept sea into perfect calm; He could multiply a boy's meager lunch into an abundant feast for thousands of hungry people; He could make the lame to leap for joy, the sick to rise up from the couch of their suffering, the deaf to hear, the blind to see, and the dead to come forth from their graves; but He could do no mighty works when the moral atmosphere about Him was permeated with unbelief.

Here is the sadly afflicted son; here is the omnipotent Christ just from the mountain of His transfiguration where saints from heaven appeared and communed with Him. The need is great; the power is present, but there must be faith. Faith is the connecting link between divine power and human need. Who will furnish faith? The boy cannot; some one must believe for him. The Lord Jesus looks upon the son in his helpless condition; He listens to the father pour out the story of his sorrow and then, ready to employ the omnipotent power vested in Himself, He says to the father, " If thou canst believe, all things are possible to him that believeth." The outcry of the father is both pathetic and prevailing. " Lord, I believe; help thou mine unbelief."

I think we can understand something of the state of mind of this anxious father. He has heard of Jesus and His power to heal the sick; hope has sprung within him that this wonder-worker may be able to do something for his son and he has brought him to Jesus. In His absence, the disciples have tried and failed. Now he stands before the Master. The glow of His transfiguration is yet upon Him. He pours out the story of his sorrow and all at once the matter takes on a new and unexpected turn. The possibility of his son's healing is thrown upon himself. He must have faith in Jesus if his son is to receive any benefit. At once he meets the situation and takes the plunge. He throws the responsibility for the healing of his son back upon the Master. " I have faith; I do believe; if there is unbelief in me, Thou canst master it and disperse it. We are wholly in Thy hands, submissive to Thy will, trusting in Thy power not only to heal but to remove any unbelief that might stand in the way of healing." This father's anxiety for his son and his close touch with Christ made him resourceful and quick to meet the situation. "Take what faith I have; destroy what doubt I may have, and heal my son." The father won out. Jesus met without hesitation the situation He had created. It was something akin to that of the anxious woman who had said in her extremity for her afflicted daughter, "The dogs eat the crumbs that fall from the master's table."

It is a splendid thing for a human being to come into a state of such desire, such intense longing, such desperation of purpose, and such daring faith that he will make the plunge, leap out into the depths, to be caught in the arms of Christ's compassionate mercy. This was a fine challenge from the father's aching heart: "I believe; help thou mine unbelief." Our blessed Master met the challenge.

The inspired writer does not go further with the story. We can guess the rest. Most any of us ought to be able to fill out the incident. The father and son were filled with gratitude. I can almost hear the father saying, "Let's go and tell your mother." And they hurry away homeward. Friends greet them on the way, but they cannot tarry. As they approach home, the mother is in the front yard; she sees them coming; they are waving their hands in the air. She is encouraged and runs toward the front gate, puts her hands to her mouth and cries out, "Could He heal him?"

"Oh, yes," the father answers, and the boy breaks in a run with extended arms to meet his mother, crying out as he goes, "Jesus is wonderful! He can do any-

thing; devils and disease must all give way and flee at
His command.  Mother, He told this evil spirit never
to come back into me."  The mother embraced him;
she looked at him.  "Why," she said, "son, you are
straightened up and look taller and larger and more
beautiful than I ever saw you."  And so he did.  It's
a marvelous thing to get rid of a devil.  It straightens
a fellow up to his full height, expands his chest, shines
out of his countenance and beams out of his eye.  Oh,
it's a wonderful thing, for the devil to be cast out and
the love and salvation of Jesus Christ to come in.

We must not tarry too long with this home scene;
the neighbors are coming in with wide open eyes and
gaping mouths to hear the wonderful news.  They ask
all kinds of questions; they are filled with amazement.
Father, son and mother are all good witnesses, and you
may be sure they are advertising the great Physician
and it isn't long till cripples are hobbling up the road,
the blind are calling for some one to lead them to Jesus,
and people are bearing their sick away to lay them at
the feet of this wonderful Physician.  No telling how
much good and blessing came from this act of Jesus.
But I must get back to the main point.

What we want to emphasize and examine is this remarkable statement of our Lord, " All things are possible to him that *believeth*."  It is faith that opens up
the inexhaustible resource of God and makes " all
things possible."  The " all things possible " is up in
the high realm of the holiest and most righteous
things; the things that bring good and blessing to men
and honor and glory to God.  All evil things or unholy

things are impossible with the omnipotent Christ. " Things " here embrace the high, the pure, the good. The things which contribute to the blessing, the help, the uplift of the lost, the rescue of the perishing. It is in this realm that omnipotence manifests itself when God can find believers through whom He can operate. Then it becomes possible to lock the lions' jaws and sleep comfortably in their den. Then it becomes possible to fling a little stone with such accuracy and force that Goliath, the champion of all evil, falls dead at the feet of a mere youth. Then it becomes possible to walk dry-shod over open sea beds, to tramp through the Jordan in safety, while the high tide of her waters stand back in awe, and to shout down the walls of Jericho. Then it is possible for men to walk unscorched in the hottest furnace that hatred can heat. Then it becomes possible for the prodigal, who has wandered far in sin, to come back to the embrace of the arms of infinite love. Then it becomes possible to enter into the holy of holies through the sanctifying power of Jesus' blood. Faith in Christ makes " all things possible." Is it not a fact that most all of us are mere children when it comes to the matter of faith? Have we developed our God-given capacity along this line? Have we made it a habit to believe,—to believe without a doubt, in humility and trust to dare to venture out upon the eternal promises of our God and claim those things which, from a mere human point of view, seem impossible?

I think that most of us have an idea that we are great believers when, in fact, we are keeping very close to the shore, limiting the power of God with an unbelief that we do not realize exists in us. We find that many Christians, out of curiosity, sometimes because of intellectual pride, read literature that suggests doubt, that cultivates unbelief, that would shut Jesus and His power up in the gospel of nearly two thousand years ago, that forgets this same Christ is alive forevermore and that He has all power in heaven and in earth. It comes to pass that it is almost a crime against the church and a scandal in the community to believe that the Lord Jesus is in our midst and that He has all power; that He will hear prayer and honor faith; that He will forgive sins, instantly cleanse the heart from all uncleanness and graciously heal the sick; that He will give us help in every time of need, that His wisdom will guide us, that His voice will whisper peace into our hearts in the darkest day of trouble.

It might be said in many communities, churches, and family circles, as it was said by John the Baptist of old, " There standeth one among you whom ye know not." Oh, beloved, Jesus is in the midst of us. He has conquered Satan and sin and the grave. He has risen and is alive forevermore. The love that went to the Cross for us, and the power that broke open the tomb of death, will hear and answer. There is a divine, supernatural power all about us, and it is the glory of our Christ to manifest Himself, to send gracious revivals with the Holy Spirit to smite the sinner's heart with pungent conviction and to draw the penitent soul by the cords of mercy to His own clefted side for salvation.

Let us wake up to the fact that we may come to Jesus; that He is full of mercy; that He will hear; the very same Jesus that restored the backslidden Peter, that so compassionately said to the poor, degraded woman found in sin, " Go in peace, and sin no more." And in the very agonies of the Cross gave salvation to a dying thief and caught him away to paradise. We can come to that Christ. We can lay our complaint before Him. We can confess our sins in the tender ear of His mercy. We can bring our sick and wasted bodies to His feet for the healing touch. We can bring our children to Him for the casting out of devils. We can bring all problems that vex us, and the sorrows that burden us, with an absolute assurance that faith will secure admission into His presence and bring to our hungry hearts and needy lives not always the things we want, but the things we need; the things that infinite wisdom understands is for our good here and hereafter.

Oh for some words to convey to burdened lives, to sinful souls, to perplexed human beings, the wondrous love, the mighty power and the gracious willingness of the Lord Jesus to help in every time of need. May the darkness of doubt pass away forever and the sunlight of an unclouded faith break with eternal glory upon our immortal souls. May Jesus become a living reality, a present, personal, prayer-answering Lord and Saviour, abiding with us always.

# V

## THE FULNESS OF THE REDEMPTION

*"Be ye holy; for I am holy."*—1 PETER 1: 16.

CONFUCIUS says, " Heaven means principle." Emerson once remarked, " God Himself cannot procure good for the wicked." In the nature of things there can be no heaven for an unholy soul. To be out of harmony with God, to love what God hates, and to hate what God loves, makes peace with God impossible, and that which makes peace with God impossible makes heaven impossible. This is not a question of theology, philosophy, sectarian prejudice or theories of salvation. In the nature of things, it must be true; it is in harmony with the inevitable logic of the universe.

It is impossible that a soul should be defiled with sin and the love of sin and, at the same time, be in harmony with God; and it is unthinkable that a soul could be in peace and joy in this world or any other world and at the same time be out of harmony with God.

The atonement made by Christ is not a provision for men to sin, nor an arrangement by which God may put sinners into heaven. The atonement provides salvation, grace and power to save men from sin, the defilement of it, and the love for it, and to put heaven into them. Christ did not die in order to provide a divine mercy that would enable polluted souls to pass through the gates of Paradise.  A merciful God gave His Son to die in order that atonement might be provided to lift sinners into righteousness, to bring them to a state of moral purity so that they are fitted for, because they are in harmony *with*, heaven.

One of the highest obligations resting upon the American pulpit is that the living ministry of the present generation dispel from the minds of the people the idea of a sinful Christianity, and that there is a divine mercy that will permit impure, unholy souls to enter with peace into Paradise.

Thousands of well-meaning church members in this nation have been taught that they can live sinful, die happy and enter a holy heaven.  They have been taught that holiness of heart and life is impossible. This is a most fearful, dangerous and hurtful heresy. Many people have been taught, and believe, that Jesus died to make it possible to admit sinners into eternal blessedness; and the effect of such teaching has been most disastrous.  The people should be taught everywhere that Jesus did not die so much to save them from hell or to save them in heaven; but He died to save them from sin; salvation from sin makes hell an impossibility and heaven a certainty.

If the ministry of this nation in all evangelical churches should at once assure the people that heaven is impossible to a soul that has not been saved from sin, and that Jesus is abundantly able to save from sin, there would be a powerful revival of religion; at once multitudes would change their entire conception of the

plan of redemption and change their conduct, bring
their lives into harmony with the teachings of God's
Word and cry mightily to Christ for the saving power
of His atoning blood.

"Without holiness no man shall see the Lord."
This is not only the declaration of holy writ, but it is
the voice of logic. It is in harmony with the constitution and nature of the human soul. It is unthinkable
that an unholy soul could live in a state of bliss in the
presence of an infinitely holy God. The whole philosophy of the plan of salvation, the meaning, aim and
end of the atonement made by Christ, is that forgiveness may be granted and that the cleansing power of
Jesus' blood may bring human souls into a state of
forgiveness, purging and cleansing from all indwelling
sin, and bring it into oneness and communion with the
blessed Trinity.

It is unthinkable that a holy God could create a sinner or that He could have fellowship with a sinner.
Man was created pure. In the use of his free agency
he chose to sin. Sin brought separation from God.
God could love a sinner, but He could not fellowship
with him. He could pity the sinner, He could provide
for his redemption, call him to repentance, offer him
pardon, provide for him a full and complete atonement, cleanse him from all impurity and bring him
back into harmony with Himself.

This was, and is, the great object of the atonement.
It was for this purpose that the Lord Jesus came into
the world. He was to save men from all sin, to cleanse
them from pollution, to take the desires for sin and the

love of it out of their natures and to set up within them the Kingdom of God which is " righteousness, and peace, and joy, in the Holy Ghost." The Lord Jesus in the atonement wrought upon the Cross has provided all that God requires and all that man needs. Those who receive the full benefit of the atonement made by Christ need have no fear of death or of coming judgment. It is impossible that Satan could put a stain upon the human soul that Jesus cannot cleanse away. " He is able to do exceeding abundantly, above all that we ask or think." " In him all fulness dwells." Unto Him is given all power in heaven and in earth. He has declared Himself able to give rest to all the burdened race. It is the high note of His Gospel. " Come unto me, all ye that labor and are heavy laden, and I will give you rest." He follows this with, " Whosoever cometh unto me, I will in no wise cast out."

Isaiah, under the inspiration of the Holy Spirit, anticipated the coming and atonement made by Christ and its ample sufficiency to meet all the needs of man, and wrote in his prophecy: " Though your sins be as scarlet, they shall be as white as snow; though they be red like crimson, they shall be as wool." John, the Beloved, looking upon the Christ whom Isaiah had seen in the distant future, says, " The blood of Jesus Christ, his Son, cleanseth us from all sin." The Apostle Paul rejoices in the fact of this redemption, saying, " I am not ashamed of the Gospel of Christ: for it is the power of God unto salvation to every one that believeth." He further says, " For the law of the Spirit of life in Christ Jesus hath made me free from the law of sin and death . . . but where sin abounded grace doth much more abound." He goes forward declaring that "Now being made free from sin, and become servants to God, ye have your fruit unto holiness and the end everlasting life."

The mission of Christ in the world was to solve the sin problem, to provide an atonement fully equal to the necessities. Sin had separated man from God. He could not be restored to full fellowship and coöperation with God in the plan of the universe and the program of the ages until sin had been separated from him. God cannot change; the sinful man must change or be forever out of harmony with God.

The annunciation angel instructed Mary to call the child "*Jesus,* for he shall save his people from their sins." John, forerunner of our Lord, pointed Jesus out as the "Lamb of God who taketh away the sin of the world." The sacrificial ceremony of the ancient priests, the proclamation of the inspired prophets, and the writings of the holy apostles, all united in exalting our Lord Jesus, mighty to save to the uttermost. This is the message of the ministry. This is the need of the world. Men must be taught the ruin of sin, the blight and destruction it brings into the soul, and the wonderful provision made at such tremendous cost to take sin away, to change man's entire attitude toward sin, to bring him to love what God loves and hate what God hates.

If beginning with the new year the ministry of the evangelical churches of these United States should declare with great earnestness and zeal that there is not, and cannot be, any harmony with God on earth, or peace with God in heaven, so long as men love sin and commit it, that salvation does not mean submitting to certain ordinances, making a profession of faith and uniting with the church, but it means the forsaking of sin, the shunning of the appearance of evil, and turning to Jesus Christ with all the heart for redemption, for pardon, for cleansing, for freedom, from the love of sin and its power,—I say if these truths were preached, this kind of redemption offered, and Jesus Christ lifted up, millions of people will flock to Him for deliverance, revivals would break out and a new era of peace and blessedness would come to our unsettled and disturbed nation.  O that our ministry would cease to ventilate from the pulpit their notions, philosophies, and opinions, and mightily preach the Gospel and offer to the people the Christ of the Gospel.  What hunger of soul could be aroused, and the lost people would throng about the great Saviour and touch the hem of His garments of power for cleansing and salvation.

We have little comprehension of the love of God which gave the Christ to poverty, to humiliation, to suffering, to the mob, to spittle, to the Cross, with all its shame and agony, that we might be redeemed from sin.  It's a heart-breaking sorrow that God should have so loved us, paid for us such a marvelous price, that our Lord Jesus should have suffered such shame and agony, and yet the untold millions go on in ignorance of the redemption provided in the Lord Jesus and the glorious possibilities involved in the full and free redemption brought to us in the sufferings of the Cross.

Among those who may read this sermon, there are those whose souls are in distress, whose hearts are hungry. Jesus is mighty to save. Let your surrender be complete. Let your consecration be without reservation. Let your faith be without doubt. Lay hold upon Jesus Christ, make Him your Saviour, sanctifier and keeper. Receive the Holy Ghost to indwell and keep you, and give you power, both to live and walk in righteousness before God, and to serve God and humanity in the beauty of holiness.

The text has in it the nature of a commandment. God created the universe. He built our globe. He created man in His own image and likeness. When man fell into sin, God's love followed him and redeemed him at tremendous cost. By creation and redemption, man belongs to God. His love for man gives Him supreme right to call him away from sin, to purity of heart and righteousness of life. The command to be holy is not the stern harsh voice of tyranny. It is not the arbitrary dictation of a selfish despot. It is the voice of wisdom and love. It is the breaking forth of infinite pity and tender solicitude. It has in it an invitation and a pledge for the highest good.

God always provides for the meeting and keeping of His commandments. He commands us to be holy, and on Calvary's rugged Cross He provides for our cleansing from all sin; the most desirable state for a human soul in this universe is freedom from sin. This freedom takes away the fear of Judgment. It turns the deathbed into a chariot of triumph. It opens wide the gates of Heaven. It is a passport to all the unfolding greatness, development and glory of eternal discovery and progress.

Come, let us listen to the commandment of wisdom, the call of love, the entreaty of compassion, the pledge and promise of full redemption and gather about the foot of the Cross of our adorable Redeemer for a full and free deliverance from all sin and that holiness which alone fits us for Heaven, brings us into harmony with God, and makes all eternity an ever-widening and rising blessing of inexhaustible life and glory.

# VI

## CHRIST DESTROYS THE WORKS OF THE DEVIL

*"He that committeth sin is of the devil."*—1 John 3: 8.

PERHAPS there has been no time in the history of this nation when there were so many dangerous and deceptive heresies abroad in the land as at the present time, and no time when people were so ready to hear and be led away by teachers whose doctrines and theories are entirely out of harmony with the Word of God.

The World War, like all great wars, was fearfully demoralizing. Many people suppose themselves to be religious and to have a fixed faith who are quite unable to stand a severe test. They have no spiritual root in themselves; they are not grounded and settled in the truths of the Gospel. Great moral upheavals and social disturbances shake them loose from what they supposed to be sure religious anchorage.

The large number of preachers who were found to be quite unsound in the cardinal doctrines of Christianity when the stress of war came upon us are no more heretical now than they were before, but the War gave them opportunity to reveal through their lips what was subtle and concealed in their hearts before the War broke out. I remember when a small boy, during the Civil War, to have heard a neighbor remark to my grandfather: " This war has made a great many thieves." My grandfather's answer was, " The war has not made thieves, but it has given thieves a good opportunity to steal." " Stealing," said he, " never made a man a rogue; he was a rogue or he would not have stolen."

False teachers whose hearts and minds were unsound in times of peace seized the opportunity when the War broke out and the attention of the people was centered upon the great issues involved, the hurry of preparation and the carnage and strife of the battlefield, to pour forth their unscriptural teachings and skeptical philosophies. The nation has not yet been able to recuperate its moral and spiritual health and the unbelievers in the great fundamental truths of the Holy Scriptures have been very industrious to improve their opportunity to draw the people away from the Word of God and the faith of the fathers.

There is another thing that has furnished these false teachers with very fruitful soil. The eagerness for church members and the race between the various denominations to report large numbers of adherents has been wonderfully favorable to very cheap and popular methods of making converts and taking into the church hosts of people who have known nothing of a profound conviction for sin and the regenerating power of the Holy Ghost which brings earnest souls into the Kingdom of God.

There is nothing more dangerous and hurtful to the Church than that she should become indifferent with regard to the things taught in her pulpits and so eager for numbers that she takes into her communion persons who know nothing of the true spirit of Christianity, who have not been brought into the Kingdom of heaven by a powerful renewing of the Holy Ghost. Such people, of course, can have no spiritual enjoyment. They have been taught that they have done what the Word of God required in order to make them Christians. They do not find the peace and joy which has been promised them by the ministry and the church. They have no happy experiences and they find themselves utterly lacking of that Christian fortitude, uplift of soul and strength of Christian character which gives them spiritual victory over temptation and the worldliness with which they are surrounded.

It is impossible to develop a strong spiritual army that can be trusted under the temptations of Satan, the ridicule and sneer of the world, if they have not experienced the regenerating power of God. Unregenerated people in the Church furnish excellent soil for the sowing of the seed of skepticism. Such people will readily become the disciples of those preachers who inculcate the seductive tenets of destructive criticism, who write question marks over the plainly written Word of God. Such people furnish excellent lumber for the mills of Mrs. Eddy and Pastor Russell. They are ready to listen to the unscriptural and illogical teachings of such men as Fosdick, Grant, and others who are denying the inspiration of the Bible, the Virgin Birth and Deity of our Lord and the need of a blood atonement for our sins. These unfortunate people become the easy victims of all manner of false teaching because they have no solid foundation of divine truth upon which to rest their weary souls; having never entered the green pastures of divine grace, they are wandering about in the highway of sin, nibbling all kinds of heretical herbage. Having not been born of the Spirit, they have not entered into the Kingdom of Heaven; they are not the children of God; they love sin; they have no divine power in them to detect it or to resist it; and while they claim to be Christians they also insist that it is impossible to live without habitually committing sin against God. John uses very plain language, but it is fearfully true. They are the children of the devil. Our Lord Jesus, during His ministry among men, gave us a very clear statement of why men commit sin. He said, " Ye are of your father, the devil, and the works of the devil ye will do."

You may bring the unregenerated into the Church. They may have wealth. They may have culture, and the influence which wealth and culture give. They may come to dominate and direct the affairs of the Church, select those ministers which will tickle their ears and comfort their hearts in their worldliness and wickedness. They may humiliate and even persecute and send away from them the preachers of the real Gospel of our Lord which calls for self-denial, for the crucifixion of the carnal nature, for separation from worldliness, for holiness of heart and righteousness of life. Such a condition of things may easily exist and no doubt in many instances does exist. You have taken the children of the devil into the Church of God and they have brought defilement and wickedness into the holy sanctuary. You may secure large sums of money, build great cathedral churches, endow schools, and have the outward appearance of great things, but you have not deceived God and you have not saved men. You are turning the bride of Christ into a harlot of wickedness, and it becomes impossible that there should be travail of prayer, the bringing forth of spiritual children and revivals of religion deep and powerful, which turn the tides of unbelief and wickedness of every sort and bring the lost souls of the people into a blessed state of salvation through faith in Christ.

We must keep before us and impress upon the people the fact that our Lord Jesus has declared that no man can serve two masters, and that he that committeth sin is the servant of sin. There is a very widespread and general notion that man, in the very constitution of his nature, is so weak that his tendencies to disobedience to divine law are so strong that he cannot hope to have victory over the tempter and walk with God in righteousness. Many men have come to believe that sin is somehow a part of their physical natures; that it cannot be gotten rid of; that the salvation provided through the atonement made by Christ is so inadequate and so insufficient that after we have used up all the grace that may be obtained and done our best that yet we are doomed to live sinful lives. I must combat this heresy. Sin is not a necessity. The sinner is in an abnormal state. Jesus Christ is infinitely more powerful than Satan. He is able to do exceeding abundantly above all that we ask or think. " Where sin abounded, grace doth much more abound." " His name is called *Jesus*, for he shall save his people from their sins."

The time has come when preachers of the Gospel ought to insist with great earnestness that our Christ is able to deliver men from the power of Satan, to lift them up into communion with Himself, to cleanse them from uncleanness, to fill them with the Holy Ghost and to enable them to walk before God in righteousness and true holiness all the days of their lives.

One of the serious faults of our times lies in the fact that there is so little said on the subject of the wickedness of sin and its fearful consequences, the eternal torment that awaits the sinner; there is not the deep conviction that ought to come into the hearts of sinners and make them to see, to feel, to hate and turn away from their sins. O that we might have a tidal wave of conviction for sin; that the souls of sinners might come to loathe and hate that horrible thing, that slimy serpent, that leprous blight that separates the soul from God, that drives out all peace, that stabs to death all holy fear, that destroys reverence, that bye and bye dries up the fountain of penitential tears and breaks and withers the arm of faith; that kindles the fires of torment within the human breast, that sets up the deep and remorseful lamentation in those immortal spirits who reject the truth, trample on the commandments, refuse the mercies of God and go through life the children of the devil and out of this life into the bottomless abyss of darkness.

We are having no little of cheap talk about the divine

fatherhood and universal brotherhood. God is not the
spiritual father of the unregenerated wicked. The only
way into the great family of the redeemed is by faith
in Jesus Christ and the power of the Holy Ghost working in man that wonderful change of heart which makes
him in Christ a new creature. Our Lord has spoken
with great emphasis and clearness on this subject.
" Except a man be born again he cannot see the kingdom of God." The whole process of conviction for
sin, the discovery of it, the loathing of it, and repentance for it, is to bring the soul into an eternal rebellion
against it. This is the very first issue to be settled
between God and the sinner. " Let the wicked forsake
his way, and the unrighteous man his thoughts, and let
him return unto the Lord and he will have mercy upon
him, and to our God and he will abundantly pardon."

When it comes to salvation we must deal directly
with God. His terms are plainly stated. Sin must be
forsaken. The soul must come into humble submission
and glad obedience. Nothing short of genuine repentance can make saving faith possible. In the things
of salvation we are not dealing with pastors who would
make a good report at conference, or some evangelist
who must have a large number of professions to keep
up his reputation, but we are dealing with the eternal
Trinity, with the Christ who hung upon the Cross to
save us from our sins and who will sit upon the throne
of judgment in that great day to come. We must go
under the searching eye which cannot look upon sin
with any degree of allowance.

Mark you, I am not saying that Christians will not

be tempted or that they cannot sin. They will be tempted, but they need not sin. I am also saying that those church members who live in willful sinning against God are not the children of God. " He that committeth sin is of the devil." The text sounds severe, but it is the Word of God and it is in harmony with the nature of things. If the child of God finds that he has sinned, he must at once flee to the divine Master for forgiveness. He must speedily repent and trust Christ for restoring grace and mercy. If any man sin, he hath an advocate with the Father, but that advocate is not to save him *in* his sins, but to save him *from* his sins. No person claiming to be a Christian should be contented without abiding victory over Satan and sin, the world, the flesh and the devil. Let us not be content without the regenerating grace and sanctifying power of our Lord Jesus and the keeping power of the indwelling Holy Ghost. If the reader's experience is not up to this standard, then hasten to your knees and wrestle, Jacob-like, until your soul finds blessed victory in our Lord Jesus who is able to do exceeding abundantly above all we ask or think.

# VII

## THE FRIENDSHIP OF THE WORLD

*"Know ye not that the friendship of the world is enmity with God? Whosoever therefore will be a friend of the world is the enemy of God."*—JAMES 4: 4.

THE Apostle James is here pointing out the cause of war, strife and all evils that beset the race and bring trouble and sorrow to mankind. The root of the whole matter is in the lusts of the flesh; that is, inordinate and carnal desires; a passion for things that we do not need, ought not to seek after, and that make human beings savages to kill, to destroy, and to become demonish in their rapacious thirst after the things of the world.

Perhaps we should here define the word "world." It is understood that the inspired writer has no reference to the globe upon which we live, but to the unholy customs, habits, pursuits, desires, pleasures, gratifications, and evils after which men seek and with which they occupy themselves. The Apostle tells us that to have friendship with these things, to seek them, to court them, to desire them, is to be at enmity with God. His words are very strong, very positive: " Whosoever therefore will be a friend of the world is the enemy of God."

We believe that we are living in times when vast multitudes of people, not only in the world, but in the

Church also, are quite friendly with the world; on good terms with the things about us everywhere which are not of God, which do not contribute to humility, growth in grace, to building up the faith in Christ, to the purging and purifying of the heart, and the lifting up of the soul into communion and fellowship with Christ.

We must not forget that there is a devil loose in our world; that he is a powerful personality of vast experience, of shrewd and penetrating intellect; that he has wonderful knowledge of humanity, of the weaknesses and natural tendencies of human nature, and that he is set on the ruin of men, to darken their minds and destroy their souls. He is a great deceiver. He knows that mankind desires happiness and it is his business to put them on the wrong road in their search after it; to make them believe that peace of mind and happiness of soul are to be found where it is not; to suggest to them false views and wrong notions of how happiness is to be found.

It is his purpose to so twist man's intelligence, corrupt his heart, and deceive his mind, that he may make him believe that the ways of God are contrary to a man's best interest, that they hurt and hinder him; that the path of righteousness is rugged and difficult; that it is an impossible path; that no man can live in harmony with Bible standards; that God has given us laws that can neither be understood nor obeyed; that righteousness and holiness are up stream against impossible currents without means of propulsion sufficient to overcome the natural gravitation of life. Thus he would create in men enmity against God. He would make them believe that the way of happiness is to drift with the general current of life, follow their natural tendencies, gratify their desires as they arise. He suggests that you do not be eccentric or contentious, but be friendly with the multitude about you. Do not be odd and fanatical, but be in harmony with the age in which you are living, the habits, the fashions, the customs of the people with whom you are associated; adopt their methods of business, cut your clothing according to their pattern, seek your pleasure with the multitude, give up contention and strife against the great currents of human thought and action. He would make you believe that it is unreasonable for God to create beings with such natural appetites and inherent tendencies and place them in such a world and then ask them to be unlike the world; to be pure in the midst of its corruption, meek and lowly in the midst of its splendor and pomp, forgiving and gentle in the midst of its self-assertion and revenge, to practice simplicity and economy in the midst of the world's fashion, show and extravagance. The devil seeks to prejudice men against God and righteousness and make them believe that their Creator is a hard Master.

You will remember that he commenced his operation against the human race in this very way. He taught our Mother Eve that God was arbitrary and tyrannical; that He had forbidden her to partake of the fruit of the very tree that would contribute most largely to her happiness, enlightenment, and progress in life. He has followed that plan of operation ever since. There are multitudes of our fellow-beings who do not believe they could make a living if they obeyed God, if they adhered strictly to the teachings of the Ten Commandments. In their deceived state of mind they feel that the world is their friend, and that God would curtail their happiness and prevent their success in life and thus there springs up within them a friendship with the world and enmity against God. They are in actual rebellion. They delight in sin. They blaspheme the holy name of their Maker, and trample ruthlessly upon His commandments. Through the ages Satan's deceptions have been on so vast a scale that the history of the race has become a great muddy stream of wickedness. Satan has so corrupted the minds of men that lawmakers disregard God and come to believe that it is impossible to recognize Him and His laws, and direct the affairs of state into channels that would bring the largest good. Satan has so deceived women that the customs and fashions in dress become ungodly and cannot be followed without hurt to the soul. He delights in extravagance. He would plunge the people into debt, and drive them into dishonesty.

Those who would be the friends of God must separate themselves from the fashions, the customs, the amusements and pleasures of the world. That host of church members devoted to modern indecent dress, who are running with the world to the dance, the play-house, the card party, the race course, and all of those inventions of Satan and godless men, who seek to secure for themselves financial advantage regardless of the good morals of the community, the peace of the home, the purity and devotion of the Church, are not glorying in the Cross; they know nothing of the crucifixion of the " old man " who is full of worldly lusts and sinful desires.  They know nothing of the blessedness of denying self, taking up the Cross and following Jesus.  They are entire strangers to the sweetness, the peace and security of a life that is " hid with Christ in God."

Obedience to the divine law and the joyful practice of the precepts of the Lord Jesus are quite impossible to those who are " dead in trespasses and in sin;" who are without spiritual discernment; who are entirely unacquainted with the blessed and uplifting power of hungering and thirsting after righteousness.  In his natural state man is friendly to the world and he will drift with its current and find his shallow and unsatisfying pleasures in the pursuit of what the world promises.  He must be regenerated in order to the breaking up of these natural tendencies and unholy friendships.  He must be transformed out of darkness into light.  He must be made in Christ a new creature and come to find happiness and contentment in an entirely new realm of existence.

It were folly to take people into the Church without the regenerating power of God and expect them to understand the mystery and blessedness of communion with Christ, denial of self and separation from that worldliness which is enmity against God.  Unfortunately, multitudes of people have been taken into the Church on mere human decision without any knowledge or experience of a powerful operation of the Holy

Spirit in regeneration. Naturally they love the world and the things of the world and their false teachers must needs bring the world into the Church. There must be shows and feasts, carnivals, pageants and all kinds of amusements in order to satisfy the craving of their unregenerate and sinful souls.

The time was when the Church with its regenerated membership stood out boldly against the amusements and pastimes that the world sought after and supplied the godless multitudes with, as their deceived and restless souls hastened to death and doom. But it has come to pass that vast numbers of worldlings have been brought into the Church, not a few into the pulpit and places of influence and power, that within the Church war is made upon the bulwarks that once separated the world from the Church. It is insisted that paragraphs condemning worldliness must be taken from the Disciplines; the rules and vows, which once built a strong fence around the consecrated flock of God, must be torn down and wolves of sin must be turned, without obstacle or objection, upon the sheep.

God has not changed. The words of the Apostle remain steadfast. Let the faithful minister cry out fearlessly though he may be made to suffer. " Know ye not that the friendship of the world is enmity with God? Whosoever therefore will be the friend of the world is the enemy of God." This is a startling statement. It cuts a broad and fearful swath through the Church of today; it reveals the fact that multitudes have somehow gotten into the Church of God who are not His friends but His enemies; that the time has come for the faithful minister to awaken deceived people and show them, out of the Holy Scriptures, that they have no ground for hope of salvation from sin in this life or peace and joy in the life to come until they separate themselves from the world and its degrading friendships and destructive practices and take up their cross, denying themselves, and following Christ daily.

O for a great revival that will uncover the deceived hearts of the pople, that will awaken the deluded multitudes, that will break the power of the sinful, extravagant and foolish habits and customs of a lost, blind, sinful, God-hating world and bring them to know the Christ in the power of His full salvation.

# VIII

## HOW TO BRING SINNERS TO CHRIST

*" When Jesus saw their faith, he said unto the sick of the palsy, Son, thy sins be forgiven thee."*—MARK 2: 5.

THE account of the healing of the paralytic as given in the Gospel by Mark is one of the most interesting of all the miracles performed by our Lord. In this, we find not only the healing of the body, but the forgiveness of sin; and we judge that this was true in every case that the faith that enabled Jesus to heal also enabled Him to forgive. There never was or is any question in the mind of the faithful about His power, both to heal the sick and forgive the sinful. Unbelief is the only obstacle that stands in the way of the mighty works of Christ.

There is a very interesting human element in the account, as Mark gives it to us, which is most suggestive. It was quite fortunate for this paralytic that he had four friends who had great faith in Jesus. His condition was such that he needed a group of believers to lay hold upon his cot and bring him into the presence of Christ. He was helpless; without some human assistance he would have undoubtedly died of palsy in his sin, but there were four men who believed that Jesus was more than master of the situation.

These men were also concerned for their brother.

They could not be content to let him remain sick and helpless when Jesus was so able to heal, and within reach of their helpless friend. Their faith in Christ, and their love for their neighbor set them going. They went after him; they assured him of both the power and the disposition of Jesus, the compassionate and mighty Healer of the sick. He was no doubt thoroughly convinced and thankful for assistance.

This faith in Christ and love for the neighbor united the four men in zealous effort. I imagine that I can see them hurrying away to the home of their sick friend; they are walking rapidly, they are close together, and are conversing with eagerness among themselves. They break in upon their friend with enthusiasm, surprising him with good news; they are all about his bed, all speaking at once and confirming each other's testimony. He is convinced; their enthusiasm and faith are communicated to him, and at once each man seizes a corner of the sick man's couch and they are away to the Lord. I judge there is no debate, one insisting that they carry him through the field, another contending for a back alley, another for Broadway, and another for Main Street. Faith and love, along with enthusiastic service, are very unifying. They at once agree upon the shortest and quickest route to bring their needy brother into the presence of the Master.

At one time, their way seemed blocked, but it is difficult to block the way of earnest men full of faith and on fire with love. The house is crowded, the doors are full, the windows are jammed. They possibly hesitate for a moment with no thought of giving up their object and at once they decide to climb up on top of the house. You understand that these oriental houses were flat-roofed, and that there were outside stairways, leading to the top of the house which was a comfortable place for rest in the cool breeze after the setting of the sun. These men betake themselves to this stairway and are soon upon the roof, locating the Lord beneath them. At once they begin tearing off the roof; directly there is an opening; and with cords they lower the sick man down upon the very heads of the throng, who in astonishment press out of the way, and the sick man on his cot is stretched out at the feet of Jesus. How fortunate for this poor fellow that he had friends who were determined, who would overcome obstacles, who would rip the roof off a house but what they would bring a helpless brother to the feet of the Master.

Jesus looks up to see where the man came from and there are four heads filling the hole through which the sick man descended. They are looking straight into the face of Jesus. Faith is written all over their faces. Every lineament beams with confidence. Their eyes are full of trust. It isn't necessary for them to speak; Jesus can see their faith. While their lips utter no sentences, their faith speaks in eloquence. It says, "Master, we know who you are; we believe in your power, your compassion, your love; we know that you can heal this man, and we believe you will. We have brought him to you for that purpose; our efforts are ended; here Thy power begins." Jesus could not disappoint these men. It was not in His infinite heart to do so. He never did such a thing before nor since through all the centuries; faith appeals to Him, moves Him, and secures from Him the expression of His love and the blessing of His power.

Jesus says, " Son, thy sins be forgiven thee." This was a surprise. At once, it awakens criticism; complaint is raised in the company. Some one who has no faith, no love, has brought no needy person, torn up no roof, at once says, " Who can forgive sins but God only? " Jesus rebuked him and said, " Whether it is easier to say to the sick of the palsy, Thy sins be forgiven thee; or to say, Arise, and take up thy bed, and walk? " Jesus was here showing His absolute authority, His Godhead, His rulership over disease and sin, and He continued: " But that you may know that the Son of man hath power on earth to forgive sins, (he saith to the sick of the palsy,) I say unto thee, Arise, and take up thy bed, and go thy way into thine house."

The man was healed and forgiven. He leaped up and seized his cot. It was not necessary to crawl out through the hole in the roof; the people gave way and let him walk out at the door.

We have here a wonderful lesson on *how to bring men to Christ*. First of all, the sinner is a spiritual paralytic. He will not get to the Lord by himself. He needs help, must have help. Revivals do not start themselves. Sinners do not stumble about in their spiritual blindness and accidentally run up on Jesus. It was the plan of God to use men to win men. He appoints His children to go and bring the lost to Him. In order to have a revival of religion and the winning of souls there must be faith in Jesus Christ, faith in His deity, His Godhead, His authority and power to forgive sins, and His willingness to do it.  There must be faith that He can and will save, not only the children, the decent people, the young folks, but that His power can reach those in the far country who have been smitten by sin, who are paralyzed in wickedness, who are dead in trespasses, who are far away.  There must be a faith that claims the worst of sinners.

This faith must have for its companion and yoke-fellow, love.  There must be Christian love for the worst of men.  There must be a holy longing that goes out for the outcast, the drunkard, the thief, the criminal, the vilest of women, and those prodigals who have wandered farthest from the Father's house.  This faith and love must be united and produce service.  There must be action; an inactive faith and a timid love that hesitate to put forth effort are of little worth.  Faith, love, effort, combination, zeal that will not hesitate, that will not be blocked nor halted, that will climb up on housetops, tear up roofs, invent means and find out ways to bring men to Christ,—these are what count, that bring revivals, that rescue the perishing, that rob Satan of his victims led at his will; that glorify God, that give Jesus an opportunity to show what He can do.

Observe that this man got more than he was expecting; more than his friends were looking for.  They sought to get him healed, but he received the forgiveness of his sin.  How like our Lord.  There is more in Him than we know.  He gives greater blessing than we are expecting.  He pours out grace and mercy abundantly if we lay our desires at His feet and lift to Him our faces radiant with faith. I have no doubt this man, once helpless with palsy and lost in sin, is somewhere today in the grand galleries of the universe with our Lord. Those four men with faith and love for capital to begin business with started things going that will go through all eternity.

Let the children of God get busy; kindle the fires of your faith; warm up your heart with love; locate the helpless; find out where the sinners are; go after them; bunch together; search them out; impart your enthusiasm to the dull, dead souls of the lost; arouse them! bring them in; overcome the obstacles; break the fence down; tear the roof off; press through the throng; let nothing prevent; God delights in a holy recklessness that will not be stopped by any obstacle. "The kingdom of heaven suffereth violence, and the violent take it by force."

There is no work so great and blessed, and such a means of grace to the worker, as bringing souls to Christ. If you have faith, and love, and religious industry, and holy zeal, you can bring a soul to Jesus; then you have accomplished a greater work than to lead an army to victory, to build a city, or to rule an empire.

# IX

## THE VALUE OF A SOUL

*"For what is a man profited, if he shall gain the whole world, and lose his own soul?"*—MATTHEW 16: 26.

OUR Lord Jesus, in this text, introduces us into a realm of values where it is difficult, in fact, impossible, for our mathematics to convey accurate conceptions.

If He had compared the value of a human soul to a splendid palace, we might go to the architects and builders who draw plans and erect structures, and get a very correct idea of the amount of money a palace would cost, setting down the figures and adding up the columns to ten, fifteen, or twenty millions of dollars; we could say, according to the statement of Jesus Christ, a human soul is worth more than all this.

If Jesus Christ had said, what shall a man be profited if he built, owned and controlled a great city, and lost his own soul, we might figure out, by consulting the proper authorities, something approximating the cost of a great city, with all its manufacturing interest, business center, residential district, its street-car system, light plant, water works, skyscrapers, and the vast aggregation of material wealth that goes into the making of a great city, climbing into the tens and hundreds of millions and billions of wealth; then we could add up the figures and say, according to Jesus Christ, a man would make a bad bargain if he possessed himself of a great city and lost his own soul.

If Jesus had said, what shall it profit a man if he gain an entire continent and lose his soul, we would then have a difficult task on our hands if we undertook to figure out, with any sort of accuracy, the value of a continent, with its great farming regions, its mineral resources, its vast forests, its railroad systems and steamship lines, its many investments and industries, its villages, towns and cities. To fix any sort of correct estimate upon such incalculable wealth would be almost impossible. It would run into the millions, billions, and hundreds of billions, and yet we would not have reached the value of a soul.

The Lord Jesus Christ was the only being who ever came out of the infinitudes and walked the paths of human life, who really knew the value of a soul. He is the only one who ever walked among us, and talked to us, who has seen a soul, who understands its marvelous capacities, its wondrous beauty and powers. When He came to our earth He saw at once that men had no proper appreciation of soul values. He saw that we thought souls were a very good thing to crowd into the dust and grime of factories and sweatshops, to wear out with incessant toil, to huddle into the deep mines of the earth, and smother with poisonous gases; to march into saloons and degrade with strong drink, that swaggering distillers and brewers may become million-aires, to catch in the traps of white slavery and send away into wretchedness, ruin, and perdition. He saw that man, in his miscalculation, thought that souls were fine things to gather from their homes, shops, villages, colleges and universities, throw them into squads, drill them into companies, form them into regiments, weld them into great armies, ship them away from native lands and drive them against rapid-fire guns, hurl them against walls of bayonets, and pour them like a human Niagara into the black pits of outer darkness.

Jesus desired to arrest our attention and awaken in us some sort of proper appreciation of the value of a human soul. He looked about Him for a comparison to convey to our minds some conception of its worth. Palaces were as nothing; cities and continents were not large enough; the world itself was too small to convey a correct idea of the fearful blunder a man would make if he should gain this entire planet, with all the wealth on and in it, and lose his own soul.

Think of it! According to the statements of the only one who has ever been in our midst with a proper appreciation of values, if you had a scale large enough to put into one end a human soul and in the other end your prosperous, beautiful little city, and then you put in Louisville, Cincinnati, Cleveland, St. Louis, Kansas City, Denver, San Francisco, New Orleans, Nashville, Charleston, S. C., Richmond, Va., Washington City, Baltimore, Philadelphia, New York, Boston, Glasgow, Scotland, London, Paris, Berlin, St. Petersburg, Bombay, Calcutta, Yokohama, Peking, China, and old Jerusalem,—one soul would outweigh them all. Not the soul of Moses, St. Paul, Martin Luther, John

Wesley, William Shakespeare, Queen Victoria, Frances Willard, or any other great intellect that ever blessed the world, but the soul of a sick and starving baby in the bony arms of a heathen mother in the jungles of India.

These words of Jesus awaken in us a thoughtful inquiry into the most interesting subject that can claim our attention. What is a soul? We should not be surprised if, after all, man is God's greatest creation. At the present time no doubt the angels have advantages over us, but they are older than we. As the centuries roll away, we may overtake and pass them in the scale of being. We notice that we were created after their creation; and we have not noticed that in His work the Lord tapers down from the larger to the smaller things. After He had created the heavens, and rolled the planets from His finger-tips, and prepared the earth for habitation, He said, "Let us make man in our own image." We have not read in the inspired Book that He spoke thus of any other being He brought into existence. We hear the Psalmist David saying, "When I consider thy heavens, the work of thy fingers, the moon and the stars which thou hast ordained; What is man, that thou art mindful of him? and the son of man, that thou visitest him? For thou hast made him a little lower than the angels, and hast crowned him with glory and honor. Thou madest him to have dominion over the works of thy hands: thou hast put all things under his feet."

We are told that the literal translation of the Hebrew is: "Thou hast made him less than God." We are also taught that angels are our guardians; and Paul tells us that we shall judge angels. Mark you, we are not seeking to depreciate angels, but these words of the Lord Jesus with regard to the value of a soul put one to thinking and wondering where man's place is among the intelligences of God's creation.

It will be well to remember that the human soul is immortal. We value things on the basis of their durability. After the furnaces of the suns have burned into cinders, and the stars have fallen like the withering leaves of a fig-tree, your soul will be rising upon the wings of immortal youth into the glorious heights of a topless heaven and an endless eternity.

The Lord has permitted us to catch some glimpses of the marvelous capacity of the human soul. Some years ago there lived in our community a young negro, an uneducated boy, whose mathematical bump seemed not to have been eliminated by the fall. He was a lightning calculator. You could propound to him the most difficult mathematical problems, and almost instantly he would answer you with marvelous accuracy. He did not understand how he did it, but he did it without difficulty. It is possible that, but for sin, we never would have had to labor with the multiplication table, or waste time with lead pencil and chalk, knitting our brows over difficult mathematical problems. We are not willing to believe that he was any sort of monstrosity, but by some mysterious means he had the remnant of intellectual power that might have belonged to us all but for sin.

Many years ago Jenny Lind came to this country.

At her first entertainment in Grand Opera in New York, the people paid large sums of money for the privilege of hearing her. She sang until you would forget that you were sick. She sang until you would forget your debts. She sang until you would forget your enemies. She sang until you forgave everybody and loved everybody. She sang until it seemed as if you were lifted into heaven. She sang until she was transfigured before you and seemed to be an angel. We believe if it had not been for sin, had our vocal chords not been jarred out of tune by wicked speech, harsh words and profanity, we would have such singers everywhere. These marvelous gifts and greater await us on yonder golden shore, when we are released from our captivity and come into our own.

Traveling the rugged paths of life, and fighting out the problems on the battlefield here, I have often longed to sing, but have never been able to bring my jargon voice into harmony with sweet melody; but I know that I *shall sing*. I feel the heavenly anthems within my breast that in yonder world shall break forth into immortal songs of praise.

The Scriptures plainly teach that when we have passed through the tragedy of death and the glorious mysteries of the resurrection, we shall rise on the other side in the likeness of our Lord. You remember that Moses went up into the mountain and stayed with God for forty days and nights, and when he came down his countenance shone with such brightness that he must needs be covered with a veil that the people might endure such glory. Suppose he had remained with his

God for a year! What must his appearance have been when he descended among the people! Looking into the future state with the prophet's ken, David picked up his harp and sang, " I shall be satisfied when I awake in thy likeness." And John, the Beloved, has written in his Epistle, " Beloved, now are we the sons of God, and it doth not yet appear what we shall be: but we know that when he shall appear, we shall be like him; for we shall see him as he is."

With these Scriptures before us we can begin to appreciate that the spiritual is of infinitely more value than the material; that the immortal is incomparably greater than the transient; that mere dirt, cinders, gold and diamonds of earth will not compare with that intelligence which lays hold upon the infinite and walks in fellowship and sweet communion with the God of the universe.

The human soul is capable of holiness. It is unthinkable that an infinitely wise and good God would create an immortal, responsible being incapable of a state of moral purity. It must be remembered that sin is not an essential part of human nature. God created man in a state of holiness; sin was introduced into his nature later on. Sin was the work of the devil. All sin can be eliminated from the soul without the destruction or hurt of any of its essential qualities. The removal of sin leaves the human soul in its normal and original state of purity and oneness with God.

This is the whole purpose and end of the redemptive scheme,—to separate from man that which separated him from communion and oneness with his Maker.

This is redemption. All prophecy, all priests and sacrifices, all the manifestations and sufferings of the Lord Jesus, all the writings of the Apostles, the great purpose and end of the Church is to bring a race, fallen and sinful, back into perfect harmony with the infinite will, and into perfect love of the infinite Being.

If an old man from the backwoods, who never saw the ocean, who never looked upon a ship, a boat, a skiff, a canoe, or any sort of watercraft, should come out of the woods upon the ocean beach and look with amazement upon the vast expanse of waves; if he should see lying in the sand half-buried, a wrecked ship, and if he should ask some old sailor standing by, " What is this object before me? " and the sailor should say, " That is a ship;" the old man from the backwoods would exclaim, " That a ship! Is that what you traverse the sea in? Can you carry commerce and passengers across the vast ocean in that sort of thing? " The old sailor would answer him, " That is a wrecked ship. That is the ruin of a great vessel that went down in triumph to the sea." The old sailor would tell him of the splendid structure, of its length, and breadth, and depth; of its staunch timbers and iron sides, its graceful masts and powerful engines, and how it plowed the main as a thing of life. Then he would tell him how the storm tossed it, and the waves beat upon it, and the rocks rent it, and the lightning splintered it, and the billows flung it, wrecked, upon the shore. Looking upon that wreck the old man from the woods would have a poor conception of the splendid strength and beauty the great ocean steamer presented before the tempest rent and wrecked it.

Just so it is with man. We have never seen a man. We have seen what is left of him. We have seen him after the waves of sin have dashed him, bruised and broken him along the rocky shores of time. We have seen him after the dirt and sand and grit of sin have been ground into him, defaced and marred him.

The Lord Jesus Christ saw him when he came complete in purity and beauty from the creative hand of God. He saw him before he gave a listening ear to the seductive voice of the tempter, before sin had stamped its foul insignia upon his spotless spirit. In that far-off day he was a godlike being. The Son of God loved him with a great, deep, eternal affection, and when he went astray in the paths of sin and ruin, He followed him. Followed him when it meant poverty, suffering, humiliation, a crown of thorns, derision and hatred, the Cross with its agony and shame. He followed him like the good shepherd, seeking a lost and wolf-torn sheep, to bind up his wounds and lay him upon the omnipotent shoulders of His mightiness to save to the uttermost.

No price, from the standpoint of the Lord Jesus, was too large to pay; no suffering was too severe to bear; no death agony was too bitter to meet and undergo. Thank God, He solved the problem. He knew the value of human souls and he drank the cup of sorrow and suffering to its last bitter dregs. Standing in the midst of sinful men, He looked back to their original state of purity and godlikeness. He gazed into the eternities of unfolding grace and glory, and as He contemplated man's origin and the possibilities of his redemption and the eternal future,—as He weighed these possibilities and destinies, He exclaimed, " What shall it profit a man if he shall gain the whole world, and lose his own soul? "

At the close of His mission and ministry here, hanging pale and bleeding on a Roman cross, He bowed His head and said, " It is finished." A bridge of redemption and human hope stretched like a mighty arch across the centuries from the fall of Adam in the Garden of Eden to the death of Jesus Christ on the hill of Calvary; over that bridge multitudes and millions have been coming back to God and home to heaven. And when the end shall have come at last, and the immaculate and ever adorable Redeemer shall stand in the midst of those redeemed by the sacrificial blood which He shed upon Calvary's rugged brow, " He shall see of the travail of his soul, and shall be satisfied."

In yonder world when we behold the unfolding development and progress of human souls,—the " exceeding and eternal weight of glory "—we shall be prepared to appreciate more fully the deep meaning of the text, " For what is a man profited if he shall gain the whole world, and lose his own soul? "

# X

## THE FRUIT OF THE SPIRIT

*" The fruit of the Spirit."*—GALATIANS 5: 22, 23.

THE inspired apostle, writing to the Galatians, draws a vivid picture of the two natures in man,—the evil and the good; the carnal nature, which is not subject to the law of God, and the spiritual nature, which " delights in the law of God after the inward man." This inward man which delights in the law of God is the *new man* born of the Spirit; but this carnal nature is the *old man* who must be endured or must be " crucified."

The apostle gives us a beautiful description of the fruit produced by the Spirit in those who are under his reign and guidance. The apostle does not say the fruit of a *good man*, but the " fruit of the Spirit." This fruit is produced by the Holy Spirit in the man. This does not mean that the man himself ceases to be a free agent and responsible for his conduct, but he, of his own will, receives the Spirit; he yields himself up to the work of the Holy Spirit which dwells in him. The result is the fruit produced by the Spirit.

Our Lord Jesus gives us a bit of very sound philosophy that will be almost universally accepted without controversy when he says, " The tree is known by its fruit." He also illustrates the truth by saying that

"men do not gather grapes of thorns, or figs of this-
tles." I suppose no chemist could give us the secret of
the difference in the nature of the sap of the tree which
makes it bring forth fruit after its kind. Here is one
tree laden with delicious pears; another is yielding
luscious peaches; another is bending its boughs under
the weight of beautiful apples. Somewhere, hidden
away in the heart and sap of these different trees, is
the secret that brings forth fruit so diverse from each
other in appearance and flavor.

The secret of a holy life of glad obedience to the
law of God, of joyful submission to the will of God;
the secret which makes the yoke of the Lord easy and
His burden light is hidden deep in the soul of the child
of God by the indwelling of the Holy Ghost, and
where He indwells the buds of life appear, the blooms
of beauty are produced, and the rich fruit of righteousness grows and ripens. This fruit, the inspired writer
tells us, is "love, joy, peace, longsuffering, gentleness,
goodness, faith, meekness, temperance; against such
there is no law."

It must not be understood that such a state of grace
delivers one from obedience to the Ten Commandments or submission to the whole law of Christ,—the
law of love—but there is no violated law, no warrant
for the arrest of any one possessed of this fruit. The
fruit mentioned here places one in such harmony with
God, and such coöperation with Him, that he is not
subject to pursuit or arrest by any high sheriff of
heaven. He walks free anywhere and everywhere in
God's universe. He is indeed in Christ a "new

creature." He is regenerated, he is sanctified, he is Spirit-filled; he has victory over himself; his appetites are well regulated and controlled; his attitude toward his fellow-beings is one of forgiveness, compassion and kindliest solicitude. He is altruistic toward all the world. He is deeply concerned for his neighbors, and his sympathies go out over all seas. He loves God supremely and his neighbor as himself. This state is not natural. It is quite unlike, and indeed contrary to, the natural man. As the sap of the healthy fruit tree flowing through roots, trunk and branches, manifests itself in delicious fruit, so the Holy Ghost dwelling in the children of God produces this fruit. A man finds his nature changed; his old desires are gone; he is possessed of a new and entirely different life; supernatural powers from another world and another personality have come into him and wrought a great miracle of grace,—a glorious change.

The apostle tells us of the lusts of the flesh—that is, of the carnal nature in the man before the change takes place, prior to the incoming and blessed work of the Holy Spirit. The contrast is something marvelous. Listen to what he has to say of the characteristics of the old man of sin, the natural products of the " body of sin," the desires that proceed from the flesh, that carnal nature which is not, and cannot be, subject to the law of God. It is a fearful catalogue of evil. Read it for yourself: " For the flesh lusteth against the Spirit, and the Spirit against the flesh: and these are contrary the one to the other: so that ye cannot do the things that ye would. But if ye be led of the Spirit, ye are not under the law. Now the works of the flesh are manifest, which are these: Adultery, fornication, uncleanness, lasciviousness, idolatry, witchcraft, hatred, variance, emulations, wrath, strife, seditions, heresies, envyings, murders, drunkenness, revellings, and such like."

Note that the conditions described here may exist at different times in the same man. The conditions are as adverse as one could imagine. They seem as wide apart as demon and angel. Those under the domination of the flesh are in a most fearful state. Those who are filled with the Spirit are blessed indeed. This remarkable change must be wrought by the regenerating grace, the sanctifying power and indwelling of the Holy Ghost. All of this is pledged and promised through faith in Jesus Christ. Outside of the Christ there is no hope for this change, but in Him dwells all the fulness of the Godhead. In Him is omnipotent power and infinite love. At His feet, the insane and violent man, possessed with a legion of devils a few moments ago, now sits with joy beaming in his countenance, clothed and in his right mind.

It is hardly necessary to say that no one can be possessed of all these excellent qualities and the fact not become known to the family, the church and the community. It may take time. There may be misunderstandings, persecutions even; some will never know; there are people who cannot see one wink on a fair day at high noon. There are those who are so blinded by the god of this world that it is impossible for them to discover any sort of consistency or beauty in the life and character of the most devout saint. Jesus Himself said, " The world will know you not."

You can not more hide the child of God who is filled with the Spirit and bringing forth the fruit of the Spirit described by the inspired apostle here, than you can hide a city set upon a hill. It is understood that those wholly sanctified are filled with the Spirit, and in them He produces the fruit mentioned here by the inspired writer. Along with our testimony and witnessing should go this fruit. If we fail to produce the fruit, we must not rail against the Lord, justify ourselves or give comfort to others who testify beyond the facts revealed in experience and life. We must not pull down the standards, but we must at once have recourse to the Christ, the source of our salvation, and the Spirit who produces the fruit. To be filled with the Spirit is to produce the fruit. We shall not make headway, in holy living and in our desires to promote a genuine world revival of religion, by finding fault with the Word of God, limiting the power of salvation in Christ, or being contented with a few scrawny specimens, when our lives should be full of fruit and the tree of our personal experience bending under a weight of love, joy, peace, longsuffering, gentleness, and all the rest of the fruit mentioned by the inspired writer.

Most of us saw oranges long before we saw orange trees. When we did see the trees we knew them by the fruit which was on them. It is possible to profess an experience that does not possess us; that does not reign and rule in our lives; but no one can uniformly

and continuously produce the fruit mentioned here
without the experience of a clean heart and the indwelling of the Holy Spirit; and, in modesty and humility, such an one should bear witness to those who
inquire after the fruit, how and why the fruit is produced; namely, by the cleansing power of the blood of
Christ, and the indwelling of the Holy Spirit.

No degree of sanctification destroys free agency.
Temptations will come, and the free agent may choose
wrongly; he may neglect the means of grace, and leak
out an experience of full salvation, yield to temptation
and fall into sin. Such a person may continue to testify to a full redemption, but the experience is gone,
and the fruit will disappear.

There can be no question but that the fruit spoken
of here by the inspired apostle may be manifested in
the life of the children of God, but this can only be so
when the Spirit indwells those children; when they
are subject to Him; when He moves and works in
them as the sap flows through the tree. Let us not
limit the Holy One, discount the fulness of the atonement, or try to pull down the divine standard, but in
meekness and humility let us, Jacob-like, insist upon
such complete cleansing, such constant abiding of the
Holy Spirit, such a complete giving of ourselves to
Him to pray in us, to live in us, to work in us, to reveal
Jesus Christ to us and through us, that we shall enjoy
the fulness of the blessing of the Gospel, producing
the fruit mentioned by the apostle.

We grant you that Satan will never be contented
with any state of grace attainable; that he will always

find fault and bring accusation. It is so with his children. Indignation against sin is not sinful anger. It is an evidence of righteousness. Excitement if one's house should catch on fire is not wickedness. Holy people may disagree about various and sundry things and each may argue his point very earnestly; this need by no means indicate a lack of purity of heart. There is no promise in the Scriptures that we will come into any state of grace in which we would all agree on every subject. Paul and Silas had a contention which was evidently with a good deal of warmth. They were honest, earnest men, but there is no ground which justifies the conclusion that they had anything approaching sinful anger or wicked designs against each other.

There are those who are very diligent in seeking out ground for excuses for themselves, or arguments to prove that full salvation from sin is impossible. Let none of these things disturb our spiritual composure or interfere with our faith. Let us hold steadfast to Christ. Let us see to it that the Spirit abides, that we keep Him in full possession of all the keys to every department of our being, and that we constantly bring forth the fruit of " love, joy, peace, longsuffering, gentleness, goodness, faith, meekness, temperance."

*Printed in the United States of America*

www.ingramcontent.com/pod-product-compliance
Lightning Source LLC
Chambersburg PA
CBHW021202020426
42331CB00003B/177